crowded around the polling place so that Negroes arriving to vote had to thread their way among them to get to the door. A new threat had made the rounds and, to make sure the grapevine hadn't failed, members of the white crowd had murmured it aloud for the benefit of the black men making their way into the polling place: "If Joseph wins, he'll be a dead man by sunrise."

Once inside the polling place, the people had to deal with an election manager who wore a pistol strapped to his hip. Many of them didn't bother to come. The owner of the largest plantation in the district had told his people, "If you vote for Joseph today, plan on moving off this place by sundown."

Now, long after dark, the word had come that he was planning to evict three families. "I know who you voted for," he is reported to have told them, "and I warned you what would happen if you did that."

When the ballots were counted, Joseph Williams had lost by a little more than one hundred votes. There was nothing obvious enough to complain about to the Justice Department, no violation clear enough to convince an official in Washington to seek an injunction in a Mississippi court.

Though he was subdued, Williams was not licked. "We got to help the people get secure," he said. "We got to help them get on a little bit of their own land or set up in their own business so the big men in this county can't tell them how to vote."

Rims Barber, the DM staffer who worked for Williams, was hopeful. "Organizationally, the campaign did a lot for this district. The people worked together, and the poll watchers stood their ground when the whites tried to push them around. The people will know just that much more the next time.

"And there will be a next time."

shacks to talk to the families. Kennedy was so shaken by his conversations with the children—one of whom had eaten nothing but molasses for the last two days—that he never stopped mentioning "the hungry children of the Delta" in speeches until the day he died.

Martin Luther King marched down through the Delta in 1966, in the last of the big freedom marches. In the nightly strategy meetings of that Meredith March, King sided with the Delta Ministry in insisting that the march's purpose be to strengthen the freedom movement in Mississippi and to fatten the voting rolls (rather than to put pressure on Congress for new legislation); they succeeded in getting the marchers to turn off Highway 51 and detour through the Delta.

And Dr. King visited Mississippi again a few days before his death, spending a day at DM's Mount Beulah Center to plan the start of the Poor People's Campaign. But it was Ralph Abernathy, along with Henry Parker of the Delta Ministry staff, who eventually led the mule train off the Mount Beulah campus and down the road toward Washington, D.C.

Mississippi has changed. But most of the change is toward the tactics of the North: still repressive, still exploitive, but more devious and subtle.

On election day, November 7, 1967, people of good will across the country were praising the victories of Carl Stokes, Richard Hatcher, and Kevin Hagan White. "It showed the American Negro what he can achieve through lawful means," announced Senator Edward Brooke.

And in Medway, Mississippi, in Beat Four of Yazoo County, a tired and subdued Joseph Williams sat with his friends and tried to see what the results of his own campaign meant.

All day long, whites, including known Klansmen, had

# The Delta Ministry

MEMPHIS
TENN.
ARKANSAS
Mississippi
Meredith march route
61
51
Marks
CLARKSDALE
Tutwiler
Winstonville
CLEVELAND
Grenada
The Delta
Sunflower
Greenwood
82
GREENVILLE
Strike City
Freedom City
Belzoni
51
'Mud City'
Yazoo City
Philadelphia
Canton
LOUISIANA
61
Vicksburg
80
Mount Beulah
JACKSON

# The Delta Ministry

## BRUCE HILTON

The Macmillan Company

Collier-Macmillan Ltd., London

Library of Congress Catalog Card Number: 69-17345

First Printing

The Macmillan Company
Collier-Macmillan Canada Ltd., Toronto, Ontario

Printed in the United States of America

TO *Ginny.*

AND TO *Steve, Philip, Tom* AND *Paul,*

WHO WERE PART OF IT TOO.

# Contents

# *January 31, 1966*

IT WAS ONE OF THOSE CRISP, gray days in the Delta, when every bush and every shack stands out clear and sharp, all the way to the horizon. The clouds hung low, tattered by a wind that whipped, unhindered by a single hill, across two hundred miles of flat rich land from Memphis to Vicksburg.

In the dim morning light, the snow piled against dead cotton stalks and collected in the bare furrows. It sifted between the loose boards and cracked windows of plantation shacks, rustling loose edges of the newspapers pasted inside.

Six miles north of Greenville, the wind rattled the windows of a guard hut, and shook the big sign on the roof: "UNITED STATES AIR FORCE—Greenville A.F. Base."

The man on duty inside leaned close to the oil heater, reading Sunday's *Democrat-Times*. He looked up now and then, peering out through the frosted windows, first at the snow swirling across the approach road and then back at the rows of empty barracks.

There was a story about the base in his paper; the Air Force was about to turn it over to the city and the state. Eighty of the empty buildings would belong to Greenville, and two hundred others to the state of Mississippi.

But the big story in the paper was weather—not that anybody needed to be told that "stunningly cold temperatures swept across the Delta during the weekend."

The story told of two traffic deaths on icy roads, and of many cars sliding off roads into ditches. In Greenville, everything from bowling tournaments to church services had been canceled—even the March of Dimes concert featuring Pete Fountain. The library had been closed because of frozen pipes, and several small fires had been set by people trying to thaw out their water pipes with blazing newspapers.

One item in the weather story the guard already knew: ice had closed the runways at the base all day Saturday and part of Sunday. Not until yesterday afternoon had Southern Airways been able to resume its eight daily flights.

At 6:43 A.M., the man in the guard hut caught movement out of the corner of his eye. He looked up to see a line of cars rolling toward him, made dim by darkness and blowing snow. Five cars, lights glaring, led by a faded red and black Volkswagen bus.

He zipped up his jacket and opened the door a crack as the bus pulled to a stop beside the hut. The steamed-up car window came down two inches, and a voice said, "We're goin' to Southern Airways."

The car started up again as he waved it on—and kept going as he jumped out of the hut and tried to wave it back. The other cars followed in close file.

He was beginning to remember that the first passenger flight wasn't due in for another two and a half hours—and that most of the faces he could see through the fogged car windows were black.

He ran around the corner of the guard hut just in time to see the Volkswagen begin to turn left, off the main street. It swung around the barrier that closed off the side street, and roared into the parking lot of the old transportation building. The other cars followed; as they parked, people jumped out and began unloading blankets and boxes. The driver of the first car was prying at the padlock with a screwdriver.

The guard ran toward the group, yelling, and then turned and ran back into the hut. As he picked up the phone, he could see the door of the transportation building swing inward, and the forty or fifty people, arms full, quickly disappear inside.

"Colonel Andrew, right away!" he shouted at the base operator. "Intruders on the base—seven carloads, mostly niggers.

"No, I don't know who they are. Or what they want. But I'll bet it's that damn Delta Ministry again."

# 1. The Delta Ministry

*"A slew-footed rag-tag of flotsam . . . from New York's slummy, dope-riddled, rape-minded metropolis."*
                                    *—Editorial,* JACKSON DAILY NEWS

ON PAPER, it doesn't sound like a trouble-making organization. It doesn't sound like an outfit that could enrage bishops, anger governors, stir up Klansmen, or cause arguments in London.

"The Delta Ministry," one of its early mimeographed fact sheets says, "is a long-term effort to end the low economic, health, and social conditions of Mississippi's poor."

It began that work in September 1964 as an arm of the National Council of Churches—an ecumenical agency made up of thirty-three Protestant and Orthodox denominations. Picking up where the short-term volunteers of 1964's long, hot summer left off, the Delta Ministry was intended to stay ten to twenty years and work on the entire spectrum of problems facing black people in Mississippi.

And despite the fact that even in 1964 the nation was beginning to lose its enthusiasm for the southern rural civil rights movement, the Delta Ministry has managed to stay alive, through financial crises, loss of support, controversy, and strong attacks from churchmen and politicians to this day. It is the largest civil rights staff in the deep South.

It has also managed to stay nearly anonymous outside Mississippi, largely through its practice of working along-side—and giving public credit to—the local indigenous organizations. Literally losing itself in the activities of a dozen other groups run by local Negroes, from co-ops to political parties, the Delta Ministry has been a model for an oft-proposed but rarely encountered phenomenon: the church-funded mission agency that draws both its leadership and its agenda from the people themselves.

Like one old European symbol for the Church—a pelican that plucks out its own breast to feed its starving young—DM has risked suicide again and again by responding to the needs of "the peoples" and "the movement" rather than to political and financial realities. It has at various times managed to alienate not only the conservatives, but its liberal friends, its administrative superiors in the National Council of Churches, and the denominational executives who pay its bills.

It is difficult to say just what the Delta Ministry has accomplished, because so much of its work is in partnership. Recognizing that in Mississippi you inevitably have more failures than successes, and that what successes do come are little ones, it is fair to say that the DM staff has worked with local people in accomplishing the following:

1. Helped register at least seventy thousand of the state's new Negro voters.

2. Operated a summer-long series of workshops to train Negro candidates to run against whites for county office.

3. Provided housing and support for Delta cotton-field workers who staged the first plantation strike in thirty years.

4. Organized sixty community Head Start committees, and found a way to get the Head Start program into Mississippi past the governor's veto.

5. Bluffed welfare officials into making free surplus foods available to more than two hundred thousand people who hadn't been getting them regularly.

6. Encouraged the picketing of factories and stores that discriminated in hiring, and of school boards that refused to desegregate.

7. Founded a new village of evicted plantation workers where black people can have full political, economic, and social self-determination.

8. Brought government and foundation funds into the state in such a way that they can be administered by the poor people themselves, and not by those whose overriding interest is the status quo.

There have been some other results—less visible, but in the long run maybe more important:

*The Church and the movement.* Since SNCC pulled out of the state in January 1965 the Delta Ministry has been the largest civil rights staff in Mississippi. Despite its ties to that cautious and bureaucratic institution, the Protestant Church, it has somehow managed to remain an integral part of the freewheeling, loosely organized Freedom Movement in Mississippi. Many people thought this impossible.

*Promises kept.* Delta Ministry has managed to survive the abrupt shift in American interest from the rural South to the northern ghetto, with the accompanying decrease in funds, press coverage, and police protection. By staying when other groups were forced to disband or withdraw for lack of funds, it has helped maintain some dim hope that for once the white man might keep *some* of his promises to the southern Negro.

*Overseas support.* This is the only project in North

America, civil rights or church, to receive substantial amounts of money from other countries. The World Council of Churches designated DM as the first "foreign mission project" sponsored in the U.S.A. by the world churches; it was intended as a gesture, but the money from overseas has in some years equalled the support from American churches, and actually kept the project from collapsing. By the end of 1967, about a quarter of a million dollars had come from church organizations in such places as Cameroon, India, Japan, Finland, Germany, England, Holland, and Australia.

*A test for the ecumenical movement.* Most interchurch ventures have popular local support. The Delta Ministry faced immediate hostility, and the founding denominations have been forced to decide whether they were willing to pay the price to keep it alive—a price that included fending off continual attacks from within their own churches. So far, they have stood the test.

*The Church and politics.* The Delta Ministry, by supporting the Freedom Democratic Party and numerous county voters' leagues, brought into the open the question of an ecumenical agency's involvement in practical political action. Its activities in the campaigns of Charles Evers for Congress and of many local Negro candidates were effective and helped build toward more successful campaigns in the future.

*The Church and power.* It is only recently that the Church has begun to accept the use of power—black, political, economic, or whatever—as a legitimate means for reaching its ends. But from the very start, DM advocated —and used—power, including the power of an organized community, and the power in Washington of the national churches.

*Interracial staff.* Although the makeup of the staff is

overwhelmingly black and Mississippian, DM is one of the few civil rights groups which still feels there is a role for the white worker. The staff is not only interracial, but interfaith and international.

*An image of the Church as relevant.* In Mississippi, the visible Church, white and black, has either stayed neutral or come down heavily on the side of the status quo. Young people are increasingly cynical about its honesty and its relevance. The Delta Ministry has let them see one arm of the Church clearly committed to social change.

*Indigenization.* The original staff was five white, out-of-state clergymen and one Negro secretary. By the end of 1967 there were seven whites and twenty-seven black people; all but two of the latter were Mississippians. And of the thirty-four, only five were clergymen. The process of becoming locally staffed and controlled is one toward which many organizations aim in vain; in the Delta Ministry's case it was nudged along by money troubles and the mood of black consciousness, but it proved it could be done.

All this adds up to an approach that is closer to the New Left than to traditional Church strategy, and helps explain the shock waves that still reverberate through some churches when the name "Delta Ministry" is mentioned. Opinions about DM vary widely, but they have one thing in common: all are strongly held.

The editor of the *Jackson Daily News* wrote that the staff was "a slew-footed rag-tag of flotsam . . . from New York's slummy, dope-riddled, rape-minded metropolis."

Alvin J. Bronstein, who headed the Mississippi staff of the American Civil Liberties Union, called DM "the most significant contribution by the Church to our society that has been manifested in this generation."

Congressman (now Governor) John Bell Williams rose on the floor of the United States House of Representatives to describe the DM staff as "pinks, punks, and fellow travelers." A Mississippi bishop flew to New York City to tell his denominational board of missions, "The project is doing irreparable harm."

And Harvey Cox, author of *The Secular City*, wrote the staff to say, "You are one sign that God is not as dead as some people think."

Whether any of these evaluations are correct or not, they aren't the ones that really matter. In the long run the Delta Ministry will be judged by the people with whom it works—in that strange, flat, rich corner of Mississippi misnamed "the Delta."

# 2. The Delta

"*The Delta will wear out a mule in five years, a white man in ten, and a nigra in fifteen.*"    —A DELTA PLANTER

DRIVING ACROSS MISSISSIPPI from the east, you twist and turn between the red clay hills for mile after winding mile. It is 120 miles of narrow road, most of it spent behind slow trucks—a dismal landscape of little farms and scrawny animals.

And then suddenly, just outside Greenwood, the road drops away. You seem to hover at the crest of the last hill for a moment, and then swoop down onto the flat floor of the Delta.

You have left the hills behind. As far as you can see to the west, heat shimmers off vivid green fields and turns the highway to water. You will drive the next forty-five miles without passing through a town or seeing a hill. The only feature on the landscape is the shack every half mile or so, weathered gray, leaning with the wind, set down on top of pilings or cement blocks with an apparent imper-manence that its age belies.

Thirty thousand years ago this was all river. The ice

The Delta (*Bruce Hilton*)

cap from the last Ice Age was melting, and the resulting torrent was gouging out a channel down the middle of North America. For the first half of its course, the ice cap had been kept within narrow bounds by hills and rocks. But here, in the last 450 miles before it reached the sea, it flattened out to a channel a hundred feet deep and a hundred miles wide.

So much of the ocean's water had evaporated and fallen as snow onto the ice cap that the level of the ocean was four hundred feet lower than normal. The river rushed steeply to join it.

And slowly, in thousands of years, the ocean filled back up. The river slowed. The rich black mud, sucked up by the torrent in the north, was laid back down by the slower, wider stream. Layer by layer it grew to be thirty-five feet deep.

By 4000 B.C. the river had narrowed to a meandering, shallow stream, only half a mile wide in spots. Forming its banks, and stretching for fifty miles on either side, was the old bed of silt—the richest dirt on earth, perfectly flat, and without a rock any bigger than a pea.

By A.D. 1538 the land was covered with white oak, pecan, and sweet gum trees, a thick forest through which a Spaniard named DeSoto and a party of 620 men cut their way. Much of it was swampy, and once or twice a year the river overflowed to add another layer of rich silt. DeSoto found the, river and planted the flag of Spain in the damp black earth. (Despite the artifacts left by mound-building Indians at least five hundred years earlier, historians, with the usual unconscious racism, refer to DeSoto's crossing as the "discovery" of the Mississippi River.)

Two hundred years later and more, when the territories were bounded and named, the upper part of the flood plain was put in Missouri, and the people there came to call it the Boot Heel. When the line-drawing ended, the rest of the plain belonged half in Arkansas and half in Mississippi, with the river winding down through the middle. Residents on both sides would come to call it "the Delta." It would be the South's last frontier.

Not until after the California gold rush and the Oklahoma land rush was the Delta finally cleared and settled. Grant's troops, trying to find a way around Vicksburg, found it still mostly impassable swamp—so thickly covered with trees that the only way through was by boat.

The Mississippi portion stretched along the river for two hundred miles, from Memphis to Vicksburg. It was fifty miles wide at the widest point, along the line that some day would be the road from Greenville to Greenwood.

The men who settled the Delta were second- or third-generation Americans with ambition and money—men who turned the rich black soil and free black labor into huge plantations. Through the 1850s, men poured into the Delta. They fought yellow fever and malaria, the interest rates of the banks in Memphis, and the continual fear that the slaves —who sometimes outnumbered the whites ten to one, would revolt.

The Civil War did not make much difference, especially to the black people; after the fall of Vicksburg in 1863, the plantations were confiscated by the government and leased to northerners. But the new operators, most of whom had used political pressure to get their leases, exploited the slaves as badly as the southern masters had.

After the war the farms had to depend even more on money from Memphis, Atlanta, or New Orleans. The pressure to raise cash to keep up the mortgage payments, plus the fact that the unskilled Negro hands could be most profitably used in a one-crop operation requiring little training, eventually turned the Delta into a huge cotton factory. Raising cotton was a simple process. The hoeing and the harvesting could be done by hand, and even the most uneducated people, including the women and children, could help.

When they were not tilling the land, the hands were kept busy clearing new land out of the swamp. Planters could mortgage this year's crop for money to raise next year's, and the old land for money to buy new land.

The result was a feudal system. The aristocracy, white, depended for prestige upon the size of its plantations, the largest in the South. Planters built huge homes on the plantations—and in Memphis where their wives dominated the society pages.

The serfs, of course, were the Negroes. They were totally dependent upon the plantation operator for their housing, which he owned, their work, which he regulated

and directed, and for their survival during the long, work-
less winter, when he advanced what food he felt they
needed (he was to be repaid out of next spring's wages).
Even the Negro churches were built, owned, and controlled by the plantation owner. The few schools that existed for Negro children were provided by the planters,
but adjusted their hours to allow the children to work in
the fields. Members of the county board of supervisors and
the key county officers, including the high sheriff himself,
were likely to be planters. Except for a few places where
their votes were considered "safe," Negroes were not encouraged—or even permitted—to vote. And the idea of a
Negro holding office was unthinkable.

The actual contract between the black worker and the
white operator changed over the years. Until the late
thirties, the system was "sharecropping." A tenant and his
family were assigned a plot of land on which to raise
cotton. They lived on the plot, planted, tilled, and har-
vested the cotton, and divided the money from the sale of
the cotton with the landowner. The cost of the seed, fertilizer, ginning, and baling came out of the tenant's half of
the proceeds.

As machinery came into wider use—especially the mechanical cotton picker—more and more planters assumed
control of the whole growing process themselves. The
Negroes still lived in the widely spaced tenant shacks but
worked for day wages set by the planter, and at jobs he
selected for them. They still could buy their winter food
at the plantation store on credit, and have it taken out of
their wages during the spring. One thing did not change
much: many of the tenant laborers, like their predecessors
the sharecroppers, hardly ever saw a dollar in cash.

As the classic example of plantation culture the Delta
came to occupy a unique place in southern mythology.

A lead article in the official White Citizen's Council magazine said of it, "As other states look at Mississippi, so Mississippi looks at the Delta." The 28,000 acres over which Big Daddy's children fought in *Cat On a Hot Tin Roof* were in the Delta. The Delta—not Memphis or New Orleans or St. Louis—was the birthplace of the blues; an overwhelming majority of the great folk blues singers came from there, including "Muddy Waters," Whispering Smith, Peetie Wheatstraw, Big Bill Broonzy, and Mississippi John Hurt. John Lee Hooker was born in Clarksdale, and Bessie Smith died near there.

The struggling farmers of the eastern clay hills and southern pine woods of Mississippi hated and envied the farmers of the Delta, who, they said, had only to drop cotton seed on the ground and jump back out of the way to avoid being hit by the rising stalks. In turn, the planters and the sons of planters, educated at Ole Miss or at Harvard or Yale, spoke contemptuously of the "white trash" in the hills, who worked alongside their Negro hands to scratch a living out of the red clay.

By 1963, when the National Council of Churches began thinking about a project to help the Negroes of the Delta, the life of most plantation tenants was little different than it had been for their grandfathers in 1900.

Ninety percent of the tenant shacks still had no running water, and two-thirds were classed as "dilapidated" by the 1960 census. The median annual income of Delta Negroes was $456. The men who could drive the mechanical cotton pickers and the tractor spraying rigs could earn five or six dollars each day, sunrise to sunset. Their wives, and their children, from the age of six or seven, could earn three dollars for the same kind of day, chopping the weeds from between the rows and thinning the cotton plants.

The two poorest counties in the entire United States were in the Delta. The death rate for Negro children between the ages of one month and one year in the Delta was four times the rate for white children there. Only one county of the eighteen in the Delta had a health officer, and some counties didn't even have a private doctor or nurse. The most common causes of children's deaths were diseases which could have been cured if the children had had access to a doctor—mostly diarrhea and pneumonia.

The place assigned to the black man by the whites is indicated in a letter written by a real estate broker in 1964, offering a plantation for sale: "The assets include a cotton gin, a grain dryer, and all of the personality for working the farm."

Census figures for Bolivar County in 1960 give another indication of the black man's life in the Delta. Compare them with census figures for La Esmeralda, the Puerto Rican slum described in Oscar Lewis' *La Vida*:

|  | La Esmeralda Percentage | Bolivar County Negro Percentage |
|---|---|---|
| Families with incomes under $1,000 a yr. | 35 % | 42.7% |
| Incomes of $1,000–$1,999 | 32 | 36.4 |
| Incomes of $2,000–$3,999 | 27 | 16.8 |
| Incomes over $4,000 | 4 | 4.1 |
| Housing dilapidated or without indoor plumbing | 70 | 90 |
| Families receiving federal surplus commodities (1964) | 20 | 33 |
| Adults over 25 who went beyond 8th grade | 16.7 | 11.6 |

Cut off from political expression, either by voting or by

seeking office, and prevented by the plantation operators from exerting initiative or imagination, the people were as helpless and as hopeless as they had been in 1900. A Negro clergyman, the Reverend George Lee, had been shot down in Belzoni for refusing to remove his name from the voter registration list; his killer was never punished, although there were dozens of witnesses. A recalcitrant, or "uppity" Negro could be jailed on his employer's word; a Negro in jail for some real crime could be released at his employer's request, if he was needed to work.

Despite the fact that the population of the Delta was still two-thirds Negro, only two Negroes in the whole Delta held public office; they were the mayors of the two all-Negro villages, Mound Bayou and Winstonville.

The only real change was, from the point of view of the individual Negro wage owner, for the worse. For Negroes, who had been necessary in large numbers to grow cotton, now were becoming surplus. In 1887 there had been a conference in Vicksburg among planters who were worried by the large migration of Negroes from the Delta. Now some planters were talking about ways of increasing, rather than stopping, the exodus. The mechanical cotton picker was making the difference. One man on a mechanical picker could do the work of 150 people in a day. The Delta and Pine Lands plantation, which once had twelve hundred families sharecropping with mules and picking cotton by hand, now had two hundred families.

The threat of a sizable Negro electorate, still nonexistent in 1963 but looming on the horizon, added enthusiasm to the planters' desire to speed migration. More than a million people had left the state during the war years, many of them to seek jobs in northern war plants. Another 325,000 had left during the fifties. But there still were more people than the planters needed. The Ku Klux Klan at its rallies was selling records of a song entitled "Move Them Niggers North."

The mood of black people was changing too. Already they were working to help the Delta's blacks stay, and to have a rightful share in the land they helped create. A civil rights movement was growing across America, and Mississippi was the seed bed; it was the place where ideas were being tried out. Amzie Moore, a Cleveland postman, had convinced Robert Parris Moses in 1960 that voter registration—political power—was one way out of the dark for Delta Negroes. Moses, a graduate student in philosophy at Harvard University, had in turn convinced the Student Non-Violent Coordinating Committee to expend half its efforts on voter registration in Mississippi. Medgar Evers had, on graduation from college, become an insurance salesman in Cleveland; though he was a lifelong resident of other parts of Mississippi, this first exposure to the poverty and oppression of the Delta had so shocked him that he quit his job to become a full-time civil rights organizer. James Meredith had entered Ole Miss amidst riots that killed two people. A fifteen-year-old high school girl named Brenda Travis had gone to the state reformatory because she sat in on the white side of the bus station in McComb. Near Hattiesburg, in 1961, a light-skinned Negro sawmill operator and grocery owner named Vernon Dahmer was helping two young voter-registration workers representing SNCC, Hollis Watkins and Curtis Hayes. He had bought them a car and let them work mornings at the sawmill for survival money while spending the afternoons trying to persuade residents to register. This association with "radical" activity had caused the Forest County NAACP to drop Dahmer as its president.

A movement was beginning. Already men had died. But it was a movement you could measure in inches.

# 3. A Ministry with the Poor

"*These colored people are not abused in any way, but the
way they're abusing us is just shameful.*"
—R. A. Ingram, owner, DAYBREAK PLANTATION

THE COMMISSION ON Religion and Race of the National
Council of Churches, organized in haste to meet the growing needs of the national Freedom Movement, was just
three days old when Medgar Evers was shot in the back.

Dr. Robert Spike, executive director of the new commission, attended the funeral as his first act in office. Later
he wrote:

"At that funeral came the first invitation—no, that is
too mild a word—entreaty, from Negro Christians in Mississippi, in the name of God, to come into that situation
where there was the kind of terror symbolized by Medgar
Evers' murder."

Aaron "Doc" Henry, the Clarksdale pharmacist who had
been a leader in the movement since he was a high school
boy, pressed the plea more strongly. The need, he said,
was for a total, long-term, in-depth ministry of service,
reconciliation, and social rehabilitation.

Within a month a small group of clergymen representing the National Council of Churches, was in Clarksdale.

The purpose, as explained in a letter to the Clarksdale mayor, was "to express the concern of national church leaders for all the people of this community, both Negro and White, in the present situation of racial misunderstanding."

The welcome from the Negro community was warm, and from the white community, nonexistent. Ministers and laymen of the white churches refused to talk to any of the visitors. So did the mayor. One local pastor issued frequent newspaper statements denouncing the visit as proof that "all the sin in the race issue was not on the side of the whites, and the Negroes are being deceived by the wrong kind of leadership."

The men were followed by police, cursed on the streets, and threatened over the telephone at night.

Fred Myers, then of the NCC's information department, remembers the welcome well. One of his best friends, a college roommate, was a resident of Clarksdale.

"I called him from Memphis," Fred says, "and he was all excited. Said I'd have to stay with him and his family, and have a good visit.

"I said, 'Wait a minute. I'd better tell you first the reason I'm coming.'

" 'Oh God, no,' my friend said. Please don't say any more.' And he hung up."

Later, they were able to meet in Memphis—but the friend wouldn't be seen outside on the streets with Fred; they did all their talking in the hotel.

The National Council tried again in August 1963 by sending an even bigger delegation. Clarksdale reacted with a court injunction against the participants.

The Clarksdale visit was the first of many failures to establish communication with the white community in Mississippi. But it put the national staffs of several de-

nominations on record as favoring the shifts from procla-
mations to actual physical presence. One denominational
official later confided, "I was told that if I got arrested in
Clarksdale, it would cost our mission board a million dollars in income. But we had to take the risk."

In a post-mortem on the Clarksdale visits, the participants agreed that the NCC had done the right thing in
going to Clarksdale—but the wrong thing in leaving so
soon. Again they emphasized the need for a long-term
ministry.

Dr. Spike continued to promote the idea in the halls of
the big gray Interchurch Center in New York City, the
headquarters of the National Council of Churches. He
found a growing enthusiasm for the idea.

In October 1963, Dr. Henry A. McCanna of the NCC
staff made two trips into Mississippi to find out what was
happening there and to sound out churchmen about the
proposal for a long-term ministry with the poor. McCanna,
director of the NCC's Commission on the Church in Town
and Country, knew rural leaders and agricultural extension
specialists all over the state. He was also armed with introductions to the young black men of the Freedom Movement—what Dr. Spike called the "most militant, most
competent, and capable young Negro leadership in the entire civil rights movement."

McCanna found reaction split mostly by color. In a
report to officials of the Division of Christian Life and
Mission, he listed the two points of view. The white point
of view, representing the most liberal leadership Mississippi
had to offer (since *most* white people refused to be quoted),
included all the rationalizations which had become part of
the white southern myth, and which later would reappear
as criticisms of specific Delta Ministry programs. Here are
some of those rationalizations, as quoted in the report:

"The battle for enlightenment is being won academically and it is a risk to endanger this victory by one skirmish, e.g., the voter registration drive in the Delta."

"Educators as well as churchmen must maintain objectivity and so can be neither integrationists nor segregationists."

"The fact that many integrated meetings could be held before 1954 and that none is officially permitted now, is evidence that the current pressure is misdirected." [This was a reference to the Supreme Court's school desegregation decision.]

"An objective review of the facts would support elimination of outside interference. The personal relationships that have always existed between whites and blacks in the South will eventually prove to be the important factor in resolving the struggle for civil rights."

"Before 1954 the Negroes of the Delta enjoyed a higher standard of living than the Negroes of any other section of the state. The lowering of the standard is a reaction to the outside pressures."

"The reaction against the NCC in Mississippi is equalled only by the hatred that is everywhere directed against the Kennedys."

"Neither the Church nor the federal government can do anything for the Delta—only the businessmen can succeed."

"The Church should confine itself to the following: (1) provide direct relief to the old; (2) more extensive education for the children; (3) set up schools and centers to help people gain the skills of good family and community living; (4) develop more outstanding Negro leadership to lift the level of the people."

Note that in 1963 the moderates were blaming the failure of interracial communication on the Supreme Court decision; a year later they were blaming the college students and the Council of Federated Organizations; a year after that, the Delta Ministry. Actually, the plaintive cry, "Just leave us alone—if you would give us the chance, we could work this out," pops up frequently in southern history and goes back more than a hundred years.

McCanna's paper also presented the Negro point of view —quite a different one. Here are some excerpts:

"The needs of the Delta are both political and moral. Although automation is evident throughout the nation, it is being deliberately employed to force the Negroes out of the Delta."

"There is, of course, a direct relationship between civil rights and economic development."

"There will be political opposition to any development in the Delta, as this would tend to encourage the Negroes to remain."

"At present Negro farmers cannot obtain loans or crop allotments and the need for cooperatives is most crucial."

"The shame and defensiveness of many white people in Mississippi offers cause for hope."

"None of the civil rights groups are willing to put enough money into Mississippi to really get at the problem."

"The power structure is not open to negotiation here as it was in Memphis."

"The only local leaders among rural Negroes are the school-teachers and obviously they are not free agents."

"There is a growing chasm between Negro civil rights leadership and white liberals."

During that tour McCanna met at various times with militant young representatives from the Council of Federated Organizations (COFO), and several representatives of the white community who had come at considerable risk. The COFO group included men from the Student Non-Violent Coordinating Committee (SNCC), the Congress on Racial Equality (CORE), the NAACP, and the Southern Christian Leadership Conference (SCLC). The Freedom Movement people urged the NCC to get going with its plan, but the whites kept urging caution.

By the end of the month, the NCC was ready to invite representatives of the Negro and white churches of Mississippi to meet with officers of the mission boards related to the NCC at LeMoyne College in Memphis to talk about the new program. Discussion was long and sometimes pretty heated, but the group agreed on the need for a program of some kind to establish communication between the white and black communities, to help poor farmers by letting them know about existing federal programs, and, by organizing self-help groups, to help train leaders for the poor from among their own ranks, to distribute clothing, and to set up community centers for adult education and literacy.

Two things made the meeting in Memphis especially important: it brought together for the first time the three kinds of people who would have the most effect on the Delta Ministry, and it accurately forecast the differences which would plague DM most.

It is dangerous to affix labels, but the three kinds of people might be called the Mississippi moderates, the ecumenical churchmen, and the Freedom Movement militants. The deep differences among these groups would threaten DM's life more than once in the next three years, and would be the hidden agenda of every official discussion of the program.

It took all morning for the group to overcome the initial unease generated by the widely varying backgrounds of those who attended. The militants included James Forman, chairman of the Student Non-Violent Coordinating Committee (SNCC); Robert Moses and Jesse Morris of the SNCC staff, and David Dennis of the Congress of Racial Equality (CORE).

There were representatives of eight denominations, and five NCC staff members, including McCanna and Dr. Jon Regier, executive secretary of the Division of Home Missions.

Sandwiched uncomfortably between were two white Methodist pastors, whose frequent written requests for information (accompanied by the spoken hope that there would be no "agitation") had resulted in an invitation to the meeting.

The NCC had to promise that the names of Mississippians who attended any of the preliminary DM meetings would not be made public. Four years later, it still proved impossible to get permission from the two white Mississippians at the LeMoyne meeting to use their names in this account.)

The question Regier wanted the group to consider was this: *What is the Christian perspective and responsibility in meeting the total needs of people who are facing a possible winter of hunger?*

The white Mississippians' response was in phrases like "move slowly," "the white people of good will can work it out," "resent outsiders," and "communication will be cut off."

Some of the denominational representatives tended to use phrases like "the need for field people of integrity in whom council delegates could put their trust," "responsible dialogue," and "respectable leadership."

And the militants spoke of justice, hunger, and crisis.

The committee came to no real conclusions. Forman presented a plan which would include field workers in various counties, a complex of training centers, a scholarship program, distribution of food and clothing, and some attempt to establish communication between whites and Negroes.

Regier and Ralph Smeltzer of the Church of the Brethren agreed, but said the imperative needs behind such a program had to be social welfare, social action, and economic development.

But each man at the table interpreted those words from his own particular point of view. The meeting ended with the time-honored note in the minutes: "Each representative should report to his parent organization, and there ought to be another meeting as soon as feasible."

A much more widely reported meeting took place in Mexico City shortly afterward, just a week or two after the assassination of President Kennedy.

It was the organizational meeting of a new division of the World Council of Churches; ecumenical brass from around the world were there, and Bob Spike made a major speech. In it he asked the world churches to help the Delta in the same way they were already helping starving people in Asia, Africa, and the Near East.

The speech had two opposite results: it fell flat with the overseas delegates, who could not understand why a rich country like America should appeal for money. And it caused a furor in Mississippi, where press reports touched off a series of denunciations of "outside interference" by the "Communist-tinged World Council of Churches."

It would be almost a year before the first project of the Delta Ministry would get under way in Greenville. The problem of getting financial support and personnel, plus the drain on resources caused by the Summer Project of '64, delayed it that long. But the critics didn't wait. They were ready in 1963.

All over the South, preachers and laymen were deploring the plans—still unformed—for the new ministry. The huge Galloway Church in Jackson, as well as four other Jackson churches, cut off its contributions to the National Council. A Clarksdale planter spoke on the Delta Ministry before a local luncheon club, pointing out the parallels between its reported purposes and the *Communist Manifesto*.

The National Council consulted the Mississippi judicatories—the highest administrative bodies of each denomination in the state. (By its constitution, the NCC is not allowed to deal directly with local congregations but must work through denominational officials.) Each official body was asked two questions: "Is there a need for a ministry to the poor of the Delta?" and, "If so, is this a work properly undertaken by the National Council of Churches?"

The box score was 9–3–1. Nine of the denominations' state leaders said "yes" to both questions (although it eventually became clear that some of them had quite different ideas of how best to help the poor.) Three denominations agreed that there was a need, but doubted the NCC was the outfit to do the job. One denomination declared that no need existed.

Armed with this report, the General Board reaffirmed its belief in the idea, and kept the ponderous machinery of denominational consultation working toward the fall of 1964.

There were many stumbling blocks. The Episcopal, Methodist, and Presbyterian (U.S.) churches were under heavy pressure from southern congregations not only to stay out of the project, but to stop the National Council from implementing it. This pressure was felt at every step of the organizational process.

Among the many influential churchmen fighting *for* the project in ecumenical circles and within their own denominations were Dr. Eugene Carson Blake, stated clerk of the United Presbyterian Church in the U.S.A., and Bishop Paul Moore Jr., suffragan bishop of the Episcopal diocese of Washington, D.C. Blake later became executive secretary of the World Council of Churches, and Bishop Moore became chairman of the Delta Ministry commission, furnishing leadership (and absorbing flak) during its most crucial first years.

Then there was the search for a director. The Reverend Andrew Young, a former NCC executive who had become Dr. Martin Luther King's close adviser and strategist, was asked to lead the new project, and gave it favorable consideration for months before deciding he had to stay with the SCLC.

It was a confusing, turbulent time for the churches, just getting their feet wet in the civil rights fight. And it was a crucial time for the Freedom Movement itself; it was the end of an era.

All through the early sixties, students had led the movement, substituting sit-ins and then voter registration for the gradual court fights which had been the strategy up to then. The students found that their strongest opposition came from that group of whites who held political power, and who thus felt most threatened by Negro votes.

During this period the federal government passed two civil rights laws (public accommodations and voting rights), and most of the organizers of that day continued to believe that the federal government would enforce them. They believed that the new laws and the new balance of voting power would lead to real changes in the social structure.

But the government did little in Mississippi to implement the new laws, and the whites quickly adapted some of the tricks of the North for watering down the vote. During the summer of 1964, one thousand young people and four hundred clergymen rocked Mississippi to its foundations. But by the next winter, the people who had risked their lives and borne incredible tension were coming to feel that it had not been worthwhile—that their methods were not going to do the job.

Frustrated and despairing, the movement spent the next year and a half in a search for more effective strategies. Many of the students went back north, to school or to good jobs. Some turned to an agonizing re-examination of the movement and the country, debating endlessly and producing position papers to be hassled over at interminable meetings.

As part of this reappraisal—and the sharp drop in funds— SNCC pulled out of Mississippi early in 1965. Later in the year the SNCC staff would vote to end the use of white organizers in black neighborhoods. Whites could stay on the staff, but they must limit their work to white people.

Meanwhile, the request made at Medgar Evers' funeral was being answered. After a year of talking, meeting, and ecclesiastical infighting, there actually was a Delta Ministry staff at work in Mississippi.

# 4. Greenville

"*I don't want the coat off your back. I want a job so I can buy my own damn coat.*"
—*Picketer outside the* GREENVILLE MILL

IT TOOK SIX WEEKS to find an office for the Delta Ministry in the downtown white part of town.

It took less than three weeks to get evicted.

"No matter what we did in that office," Thelma Barnes remembers, "we couldn't do right."

Mrs. Barnes, a former administrative assistant at the air base, had been the first Greenvillian, and first Negro, the DM hired. She was receptionist and secretary for the four other staff members: Art Thomas, Warren McKenna, Larry Walker, and Wilhelmina Rowland.

"We kept the blinds closed because the window faced south, and the sun was hot," Mrs. Barnes says. "But the women in the office across the street complained. They said we must be doing something bad, to have the blinds closed all the time.

"So we opened the blinds. Then they complained because everybody who came by could see me. They said the

Delta Ministry was flaunting a Negro secretary in everybody's faces."

It was no joke. A solemn delegation of white clergymen even called upon Art, asking that Thelma be fired. "You're hurting your cause," they said. "You're rubbing people the wrong way."

When Art refused, the good men of the cloth urged that she at least be moved into a back room, where people couldn't see her.

They went away disappointed, and a little puzzled at the refusal. A few days later, Maynard Wilzin, the real estate dealer, came into the office and delivered an eviction notice.

It was, of course, a nervous time for Greenville. The long, hot summer of 1964 was just ending, and most of the hundreds of college students who had come down for Mississippi's most traumatic summer in a hundred years were on their way back to school. All summer long, the state's image had been subjected to unfavorable national press coverage.

And it wouldn't quit. The day Warren McKenna arrived from Jackson to become director of the Greenville project was also the day the FBI dug up the bodies of Goodman, Chaney, and Schwerner from under a dirt dam in Neshoba County.

The Goldwater-Johnson campaign was in full swing, and every press or TV reference to the upcoming election was a raw reminder to Mississippians of the "betrayal" of the South by its own party. (Johnson was to get 13 percent of the Mississippi vote.)

The Democratic convention had also kept the state in the national spotlight; the only real action at Atlantic City had been the challenge to the Mississippi delegation by the MFDP. There was extensive coverage.

Mississippians feel the nation has always been unfair to them anyway. A wire-service story in the *Delta Democrat-Times* in August 1965 told about a Jackson resident who had been arrested in Virginia for having on his car a false set of plates—*given to him by the Hinds County (Mississippi) sheriff's office!* "He had," the story said, "one of several out-of-state tags kept by the sheriff's office here for lending to motorists afraid to drive in the north with Mississippi plates."

Except for the Greenville paper and one or two others, the press inside Mississippi did little to correct the picture of a beleaguered, misunderstood state.

In Pike County, where there were nineteen bombings of Negro homes or churches in September, the editor of the *Magnolia Gazette* wrote: "Pike county and a number of other Mississippi counties have had new experiences with three forms of activities completely foreign to our State— hate-mongers, bombings and church burnings."

Since Mississippi had never had any of these before, Gibson suggested, the bombings and burnings must be the work of civil rights workers, who had "resorted to the old Communist techniques of creating fear in the hearts and minds of those whose cause they pretend to champion, by committing acts of violence which all responsible citizens resent. So, they must be removed from our county and state."

In a signed column next to this front-page editorial, Gibson commented that "in the November election, the Communist forces, in and outside the USA, have made it crystal clear they want President Johnson elected. Therefore a vote for Johnson must be considered a vote for and in favor of communism."

The residents of Greenville tended to be even more sensitive than most Mississippians about their image. Greenville, they felt, was different, and they didn't like being lumped together with the rest of the state in the stories about the race situation.

There was some justification for this.

Greenville had the best-trained (some said the *only* trained) police force in the state. And if the policemen had no love for civil rights workers, they were at least determined that there would be no violence directed at them; the image of Greenville was at stake. There even were four Negroes on the police force.

There had been no strong Klan organization in Greenville for more than thirty years, since a crucial election in which the plantation aristocracy had fought—and beaten—a Klan candidate for sheriff.

Greenville writers, a visitor quickly learns, have written fifty-six books. The streets in the Negro part of town are paved—a rarity in Mississippi. A Greenville jury was the first (and, at that time in 1964, still the only) in Mississippi to acquit a Negro accused of raping a white girl.

Much of the credit for the difference in Greenville is given to the *Delta Democrat-Times*, founded by Hodding Carter, Jr., (with the help and instigation of the plantation owners) at the time of the anti-Klan fight in the thirties. Carter put the competing paper, a segregationist sheet, out of business; later he won the Pulitzer Prize for a series of editorials attacking the Klan. He has written many books and hundreds of articles, including eight pieces for major national magazines which extol the virtues of Greenville.

By the time the Delta Ministry arrived, however, Carter's health was poor and he was having severe trouble with his eyes. A son, Hodding Carter III, was in Washington working for the Johnson campaign, but would return after election day to become editor of the paper.

The town served by the *Delta Democrat-Times* (or

DDT, as everyone, including its employees, called it) has about 47,000 residents. About 42 percent are Negroes. It is the largest town in the Delta, which gives some idea of the rural character of the area. An L-shaped bay, once a bend in the Mississippi and still connected to it, makes Greenville the busiest river port between St. Louis and New Orleans.

A relatively alert Chamber of Commerce had helped Greenville lasso a couple of new factories, but none recently. In fact, the town hadn't had a new plant in more than two years, and the leadership blamed the "unfair publicity over civil rights." In this respect Greenville was like most other Mississippi towns. Prospective employers *were* edgy about getting involved in the state's racial troubles, and the industrialization program was hurting.

So was the tourist business along the Gulf Coast, which had dropped 50 percent after the discovery of the three bodies in the dam. The common reaction to the Neshoba County murders was to blame unfair publicity—not Mississippi's racial troubles. Before the bodies had been found, many white citizens of the state had believed that the disappearance was a trick, to gain sympathy for the civil rights movement. Now that the evidence was in, most still blamed the three young men, for coming to Mississippi in the first place.

And the most nervous people of all in image-conscious Greenville were the clergymen. Ever since the first announcement of an outsiders' ministry to the Delta poor had been made more than a year earlier, the local clergymen had been assuring their flocks that they had nothing to do with its coming.

Their jobs were at stake, of course, in a state where scores of ministers had been forced from their pulpits for real or imagined sympathy with the civil rights movement.

But money was also at stake. In the connectional churches, local pastors are responsible for raising a designated amount to be passed on to the state and national church offices; inability to meet the quota is a black mark on a man's record and a hindrance to promotion. The pastors of Greenville knew that some of their members had already cut their contributions because they suspected that their denominational money might somehow end up in the coffers of the National Council of Churches.

Most laymen didn't even trust their own denominational officials. Methodists especially felt that the series of statements on racial justice flowing out of headquarters was a betrayal of unspoken promises. "What's black and white and red all over?" went one bitter joke; the answer was, "the Methodist Church."

In this kind of atmosphere, nobody cheered the arrival of an organization which might bring even more nationwide attention to the Delta and to Greenville. The Delta Ministry never did find another office in "white" Greenville. The location had been chosen deliberately, to help keep communication open with the white residents, and there was a serious attempt to find another place.

Art Thomas learned that the eviction had taken place without the knowledge of the office building owner, who lived in Memphis. But this worthy, subjected to pressures from the segregationists and from a number of friends in the National Council in New York, finally decided it would be too much trouble to intervene. He refused to reverse the eviction order.

The DDT ran an editorial headed "This Isn't Greenville." It charged that "there are at least some rental property owners in Greenville who are personally willing to rent to the DM's staff, but who are afraid to do so because of overt or covert pressure.

"Our community has a precious heritage of dissent, of going our own way no matter what others in the state might do," the editorial said. Now, "there is evidence that Greenville is giving ground to those who would strait-jacket us into a city of conformists."

It didn't work. Neither did an ad the staff bought in the paper:

LET GREENVILLE KNOW

The Delta Ministry is being forced out of its office at 236 Washington Avenue.

Why?

Because we are a project of the National Council of the Churches of Christ in America working with all churches and both races.

Is there any white person with the moral courage who will rent us office space in the downtown business district? If so, please telephone 335–1213 or 334–4935.

Nobody answered the ad. And the Greenville project, which many times in the future would be accused of having by-passed the white community, moved into the Negro part of town where it belonged.

But finding a place to work didn't take much of the staff's time. Most of them didn't work in an office anyway.

Larry Walker, a quiet, sandy-haired Baptist minister from Georgia, spent the first two months listening—in the Negro community. He attended church meetings and he sat around in juke joints. He ate in Negro restaurants and shot pool in the Negro pool hall. He attended the Thursday night rallies left over from the COFO summer. And as people learned to trust him (the idea of a white man who listened, rather than talked, took some getting used to),

Larry began to learn the real needs and real concerns of Greenville's black citizens.

"Billy" Rowland, a gracious, gray-haired southern lady with traces of her native Georgia still in her speech, was also listening. She rented an apartment—after considerable delay and trouble—in one of the better white residential neighborhoods. She furnished it beautifully (the screams from the NCC accounting department in New York still echo across the Hudson) and began to invite Greenville's most liberal people for evenings of conversation, cocktails, and coffee.

Miss Rowland, an ordained Presbyterian minister who had been a missionary to China and a professor at the University of North Carolina, had the job of making white Greenville understand what the Delta Ministry was doing.

McKenna, a forty-six-year-old Episcopal priest, had spent the summer in Jackson administering the work of four hundred visiting clergymen under conditions which ranged from utter confusion to downright danger. This was good preparation for setting up a Delta Ministry office. He was the phone link with McComb, where a project was growing out of the response to the bombings, and with Hattiesburg, where the Presbyterian Church had had a project for nearly a year.

The DM's field director, Art Thomas, was on the road. There was always to be some impending institutional disaster requiring his presence in Washington, New York, Atlanta, or Jackson. He was trying to build a staff, establish liaison with some of the more bureaucratic types in the NCC headquarters, find more budget money, and draw up a program for his new organization. (Typical of the crises that autumn was the announcement in November by the Presiding Bishop of the Episcopal Church, encouraged by Mississippi Episcopalians, that the church could not endorse or support the Delta Ministry. It wasn't the kind of organization they had thought it would be when they originally approved it, the bishop reported.)

Those who were worried about DM being an activist successor to COFO must have breathed a sigh of relief during that November and December. All the DM seemed to do at first was hold meetings and talk.

There was a series of meetings in the Negro community to discuss school desegregation, and a committee was formed to meet with the school board. DM called a meeting of Negro women who were concerned about employment. The women formed themselves into the Washington County Employment Committee. The DM staff was invited to send two representatives to the executive board of the Herbert Lee Memorial Community Center—a coalition of a number of Negro organizations—and DM gave $2800 toward remodeling the center. Larry Walker was even meeting one night a week with plantation workers in the Tribbett area, ten miles east of Greenville.

In the meetings it was becoming increasingly plain that Greenville was not quite up to its image.

The hospital and all the white doctors' offices were strictly segregated. The Negro library was small and crowded; there was only half a seat on the toilet. The schools, though they were probably the best in Mississippi, were spending $134.43 above the state minimum for each white pupil—and $34.25 above the minimum for each Negro child.

Housing in the Negro area was bad. The same whites who proudly pointed to the paved streets would write three years later, in an application for federal money in the model cities program, that 38 percent of Greenville's citizens lived in conditions of "extreme blight and overcrowding." People paid high rents for three-room "shotgun" shacks built fifty years earlier and crowded together on tiny lots. "Most of the city problems of poor sanitation, poor health, poor education and unemployment are concentrated in these areas," the city fathers would write in their application.

Some of the discriminatory practices in Greenville were just ridiculous. One drugstore removed the stools at its luncheon counter after the public accommodations act was passed. Booths and tables were set up in a room just behind the counter, with a sign, "Employees Only." If you were white, the proprietor was likely to invite you back to the "employees' lounge" to eat what he sold you. If you were black and you insisted on buying, you stood at the counter to eat.

The law made service station operators remove the signs from the three rest rooms most stations have: "White Women," "White Men," and "Colored." So the operators just put locks and numbers on the doors; they could look a customer over and give him the key for the toilet they thought he ought to use.

The Paramount Theater used a most ingenious arrangement to comply with the law: two entrances. There was a front entrance, with a white cashier, and a one dollar admission price. Around the corner was a side entrance, with a Negro cashier who charged only fifty cents; it led only to the balcony. The whites paid the dollar to preserve their way of life; the Negroes climbed to the balcony with fifty cents in change. But the result was still segregation.

The World War II Memorial, resplendent in red, white, and blue tile at the end of Washington Street by the levee, with an American flag waving overhead, was another constant reminder to Negroes of their "place." It has no names on it; the town fathers couldn't figure out how to put the names of the Negro dead on the memorial alongside the whites' without causing a furor.

But all these things, though humiliating, did not cause as much resentment as the one area of discrimination about which people complained most: employment. This was where prejudice showed up most clearly, and hurt most.

The closing of the air base two years earlier was still being felt in the local economy. And the growing use of mechanical cotton pickers hurt. It meant that the children and old folks could no longer supplement the family income by riding a bus out to some plantation to work fourteen hours for three dollars during the picking season.

With jobs so scarce, employers could set their own rates; the going wage for a maid was $13 for a six-day week. White folks, especially those with maids, had little inclination to question the system, although it forced a mother to leave her own children at home and take care of Miss Ann's for $2.18 a day so Miss Ann could work downtown for $60 a week.

There were just one or two Negro clerks in the whole downtown shopping section, which served the Delta for forty miles in each direction. And these were not permitted to handle cash or touch the cash register.

The meetings revealed to the DM staff that northern-owned factories in the area practiced exactly the same kind of job discrimination as local businesses—using Negroes only in the most menial jobs. Especially exasperating to the women was the Greenville Mill, which was making carpets for Sears, Roebuck and for the federal government.

The mill, Greenville's biggest factory, had been installed a dozen years before in a $4,750,000 building erected by the city of Greenville under a state law designed to encourage new industry. To get the bond issue passed for the money, the city had waged a campaign for Negro votes;

they promised that the plant would hire fairly, without racial discrimination.

But by the fall of 1964, the people told Larry Walker, the only Negroes employed there, a handful, were janitors or "catchers" at the ends of the big looms. The jobs which paid best, the production jobs, all went to white women.

The Washington County Employment Committee, with Larry Walker and Mrs. Barnes as active members, had been investigating the Greenville Mill situation. They found that the mill employed about 1,100 people, of whom 200 to 250 were Negro men. Not a single black woman worked in the mill, although about 300 white women worked at production jobs paying $60 to $80 a week.

The Negro men were in the lowest job classifications and received the lowest pay. It was obvious from the status of black men who had excellent work records covering ten years that there was no chance of being upgraded.

The mill had been a long-standing source of grievance in the black community, an obvious example of the white man's refusal to keep his word; now the black community was ready to change the situation. Besides continuing to gather data about current practices, the WCEC took these steps:

1. Organized Negro women to fill out applications for work at the mill (and got so many to do so that the personnel office refused to give out any more application blanks).

2. Persuaded a committee of local white businessmen to meet with the plant's management to talk about ending discrimination.

3. Turned over to the federal government affidavits showing that the plant was flagrantly in violation of the non-discrimination clauses in its federal contracts.

4. Through DM and NCC's New York office, tried to reach the parent company, Mohasco Industries, and get them to bring about a change.

The contacts with the government brought the discovery that the General Services Administration had already investigated the mill's employment situation a year earlier, and had come up with the same findings of discrimination. But shortly afterward, on the promise that there would be improvement, GSA had awarded the mill a new contract worth more than a million dollars!

The contacts with Mohasco Industries in New York were disappointing, too. In the discussions, company officials used a phrase DM was to hear many more times from northern firms with plants in the South: "We have to comply with local custom." Mohasco not only refused to agree to a change in hiring; it wouldn't admit that one was needed.

True, six Negro women were hired early in January. But the word was circulated to the white employees, who were protesting, that there would be no more black women hired. It was understood that this token hiring was necessary for renewal of the federal contract, which was due in March, and that the government would be satisfied with this "progress."

On January 6, the Chamber of Commerce announced that its Industrial Foundation was naming the Greenville Mill "Best Plant of the Year." Herbert Shuttleworth II, president of Mohasco Industries, would come to Greenville to receive the award.

To the black community, and especially to the employment committee, it was a slap in the face. They had tried all the normal channels to right a wrong which had existed openly for eleven years and got nowhere. Now the white leadership of Greenville was deepening the insult by expressing its support for the mill.

The committee announced that when Shuttleworth came to town, they would picket the mill.

A few days later, Shuttleworth announced he would not be able to make the trip after all.

And at dawn on January 19, the day Shuttleworth had been scheduled to get his award, thirty-seven pickets appeared and began marching around the spacious green lawn which surrounded the plant. Shocked white employees couldn't believe what they saw, and at least one woman was seen crying as she went in to work. Another fine old Greenville tradition, that of the good Negro who knew his place and was happy in it, had suffered a serious blow.

The picketing went on for three months. COFO and Delta Ministry volunteers joined the line each day, but it was always predominantly local Negroes. Greenville got used to the idea of the pickets, and Chief Burnley's police provided protection to the marchers, mapping out a prescribed route they could follow to the mill. On a couple of days the picket line was set up outside the home of W. T. Wilcox, the general manager of the plant, bringing clucks of disapproval from the newspaper. Late in March, the group voted to go to the mill by a different route each day, in order to recruit more marchers. Told by police to follow the old route "for their own safety," the marchers refused and were arrested—twenty-six of them in three days.

During this time the mill officials refused to meet with the Washington County Employment Committee—not so much because of the racial aspects of the problem, a white Greenville leader told me much later, but because to negotiate with *anybody* might open the door to unionization. (The Delta Council, in its pamphlet for industrialists who might move to the area, boasted: "Of the more than 90 manufacturing facilities currently operating in this area, only six are unionized." If unions got a foothold in the Delta, one of the strongest arguments for attracting industry to the area would disappear.)

But in mid-April, after the WCEC sued the mill and the City of Greenville in federal court to force a change in hiring, and after several national publications carried stories on the picketing, officials of Mohasco agreed to negotiate. The long series of talks were complicated by the city's successful attempt to split the Negro group by designating who would be on the WCEC negotiating committee. Eventually, though, the company agreed that half the women working on the looms should be black, that the snack area should be desegregated, that black men should have a chance to be upgraded, and that the "white" and "colored" signs should come off the drinking fountains.

More important, the whole process had shown the Negro community that when they organized to use the levers of public opinion, federal law, and fear of economic loss, white people could be moved.

This determination grew in the next few months as the black community continued to push for change. People who had never publicly expressed their feelings were speaking at freedom rallies and marching on picket lines. People who had always been told what was good for them were now on committees which gave voice to their own ideas about what was needed.

A DM newsletter reported some comments heard along the picket line at Greenville Mill one rainy day:

"We won't get freedom sitting at home watching Amos and Andy on the TV.

"If you was going to Miss Ann's to cook her dinner, you would be walking in the rain."

The next few months saw more incidents expressing the black community's dissatisfaction with the way things were in Greenville:

Governor Johnson was to come to Greenville to present the city with an All-Merit Award, signifying it had met standards for improvement in ten areas, including library, hospital, schools, and street lighting. But the Negro community had not been touched by most of the improvement; the Negro branch library didn't even have periodical racks or a place to read, the general hospital was segregated and notoriously discriminatory, and the Negro high schools had no lab equipment for science classes. They decided to picket the ceremonies at which the award was to be presented by Governor Paul Johnson. They did; Governor Johnson never showed up, pleading "business"; the image-conscious leaders of Greenville got angrier yet.

The WCEC, after an investigation of hiring practices in downtown stores, voted to picket and call for a boycott on a newly opened discount store, the Stein Mart. They might have picked any store, since all of them discriminated, but apparently chose Jake Stein's as most vulnerable to a boycott because it was so new and because it had a very high percentage of Negro customers. The move roused more than the usual amount of hostility and criticism in the white moderate community because Jake Stein was a warm-hearted, friendly man who had been aiding poor Negro people—especially with a fund to buy glasses for children—for years. His friends blamed the boycott on the Delta Ministry. And they charged that Stein was being asked to discharge a member of his own family as a cashier in order to replace her with a Negro. (Stein confided to a young lawyer, a Delta Ministry volunteer whose aid he sought in trying to end the boycott, that the real request was quite moderate—the training of a Negro clerk so she might take a cashier's job if one became vacant. And he admitted that fear of a counterboycott by the Klan was the only thing which kept him from agreeing.) The fact remains that it was a questionable choice the committee made; a general boycott was tried a year later and was much more successful.

Black people picketed the school administration building, protesting the fact that in eleven years since the Supreme Court's desegregation ruling, the Greenville system had not desegregated a single classroom.

When the board did submit a "freedom of choice" plan for desegregation—as much a result of renewed federal pressure as of the picketing—local Negroes and Delta Ministry volunteers visited every Negro home in Greenville, urging parents to sign their children up for white schools for the coming year. The result was the transfer of 146 children; this was less than 5 percent of the black children in town, but it made Greenville the most integrated school system in the state.

Hoping to avoid a mass invasion of federal voting registrars, the state administration got a majority of voters in a special election to change the Mississippi constitution, greatly simplifying the registration process. The old eighteen-question form gave the registrar the power to judge whether an applicant had passed or not; the new form had only six questions, determining mostly whether the applicant had lived long enough at his present address and had no felony record.

One of those who came to the courthouse in Greenville was a lady 105 years old. She had been born a slave in Virginia, but came to Mississippi at the age of four "when my folks was sold to a man in Hinds County," she explained. "My sister and I was thrown in on the deal." Inside the clerk's office, it became apparent that she couldn't read well enough to fill out the form or even sign her name. She was turned down.

"I waited a long time for this," she said as she left the courthouse on her daughter's arm. "There was no schools for us, even after the white folks stopped fighting each other and we got the freedom. Somehow, it don't seem like it's my fault I can't read."

The black community responded by going again—and again and again—to every black family in town, urging all the eligible members to register.

The program doubled the number of Negro voters in Greenville during the summer, and shook up the local whites so much that they hired a former sheriff to head a new organization called VERA (Voter Education and Registration Association). Though it had the backing of the service clubs, the white veterans' organizations, and the town fathers, it failed to reach its goal—which, admittedly, was to keep the number of white voters way out ahead of the Negroes.

In each of these situations, the question came up: "What is the role of the Delta Ministry?" Most whites assumed that DM planned every incident and directed each move. "Why did the Delta Ministry pick on Jake Stein?" "The Delta Ministry is driving away new industry by crucifying the Greenville Mill." "Our people were happy until you stirred them up."

Such assumptions were based on the belief that black people don't have enough brains to decide and plan anything for themselves. It's the same mentality which sees a communist plotter behind every attempt by the poor to change society.

There is no doubt that Larry Walker, Warren McKenna,

and, increasingly, Thelma Barnes, were in the midst of the action. They stimulated, they came up with suggestions, they asked questions, they made speeches, when invited, at the weekly rallies. But in each case, they were among many others who did the same. They had only one vote each, and often were voted down; sometimes they voted on opposite sides of a committee matter. They believed fervently, almost mystically, in the need for the local people to determine their own destiny, and when the DM staffers made a mistake, it was usually on the side of not saying enough.

The determining factor in the ferment in Greenville that spring was not the Delta Ministry. It was an idea whose time had come. It was the growing awareness among black people that a better life was within reach, and a growing determination to fight for it. It was the news from Selma

DM staffers outside the state office: Burnett Jacobs, Solomon Gort, Owen Brooks, Clarence Hall (*Toge Fujihira*)

that men were dying and being beaten for the right to vote. It was the feeling that sitting and waiting for whites to "do right" was futile; it had been tried without success. The changes in black Greenville might not have come as soon or as fast without the Delta Ministry, and they might not have always been as well organized or financed, but they would have come. The aim of the Delta Ministry, emphasized repeatedly by Arthur Thomas, was to help the *people* do what *they* wanted to do.

The *Democrat-Times*, in an editorial after the All-Merit Award incident, showed that it recognized the new mood. The writer called upon his readers to "note carefully how drastically the makeup of those who are demonstrating has changed. Where once the civil rights picket lines here were made up almost entirely of outside civil rights activists plus local juveniles, the number of adult demonstrators has been going up significantly. On Monday, these were also joined for a few minutes by some of the established local Negro leaders. The symbolism of this show of unity should not go unnoticed, for it says much about what could lie ahead."

The same kind of thing was happening in other Mississippi towns. (In McComb, for example, five hundred Negroes registered in two weeks.) The catalyst might be the Summer Project, or the decision of a student to stay on and keep the COFO house open, or the return home of a black army veteran who was in no mood for the "old way," or the news about the new voting rights bill, or an active Freedom Democratic Party chapter. Sometimes it was the long-delayed willingness of people to follow someone who had been telling it "like it is" for years—like Fannie Lou Hamer in Sunflower, Amzie Moore in Bolivar, E. W. Steptoe in Amite County. And in some places, it was the presence of a Delta Ministry staff member.

Solomon Gort, a tall, lanky American Baptist minister

who had been born in Cleveland, Mississippi, joined the staff—at first to work with fellow black ministers, and then to open a new DM project in Tallahatchie County. Three nurses, Jo Disparti, Phyllis Cunningham, and Linda Dugan, were starting a demonstration health project in Holmes County. Fred Lowry, graduate of Dartmouth and the Yale Divinity School with graduate work at the Ecumenical Institute in Switzerland, had been a volunteer in McComb the summer before and now was back to stay. Owen Brooks, an electronics engineer from Boston, opened the Bolivar County DM project in a tiny blue house in Cleveland. Al and Marge Winham had left the parish ministry in New England after thirty years to open up Mount Beulah, the battered old college campus just leased to DM by the Disciples of Christ as a conference center.

One of the more spectacular additions to the staff came

Al Winham, Art Thomas (*Ken Thompson*)

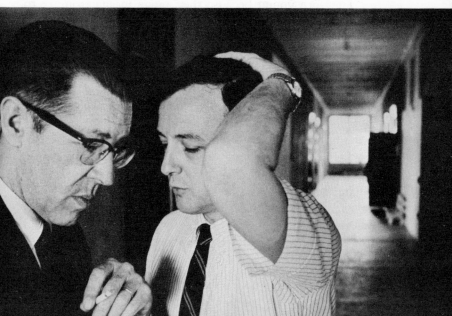

en masse, in the form of the Freedom Corps. This was a group of young black Mississippians, ranging in age from seventeen to twenty-three, recruited and trained by DM to work as community organizers. Many of them had had their first contact with the movement during the summer of 1964 and were now looking for ways to stay involved in it, for the Freedom Houses where they had found so much excitement that hectic summer were closing down.

Curtis Hayes, himself only twenty-three but already a long-term veteran of the movement in Mississippi, joined the Delta Ministry staff as director of the Freedom Corps. From 1961 to 1963 he had been a SNCC field secretary; he and Hollis Watkins were the first two people to try a sit-in in McComb, and the first regular SNCC workers in the state.

Hayes described his Freedom Corps members in a staff report as "young, energetic, radical, inexperienced and uninformed rebels.

"They are young because they range in age from 17 to 23; energetic because there is never a tired moment in any setting, be it baseball, basketball, discussions, fighting, picketing or going to jail; radical because there is not one thing short of killing themselves they won't do; inexperienced and uninformed because these young black Mississippians who for a year or more thought they were involved in the movement had to face the hard cold fact that the movement had left them out in the cold.

"As many times as they had 'gone to jail for the movement,' the movement had neglected to tell them why."

The first call for volunteers, in April 1965, was a disaster. It attracted fifty young people interested mainly in the reports of free food, free lodging, free booze, and free women at Mount Beulah (reports, ironically, circulated originally by white opponents of the movement who concluded that an integrated, coeducational conference grounds could have little purpose other than immorality). Though they were presented with an ambitious curriculum that included Negro history, leadership training, group dynamics, and the practice of nonviolence, the volunteers spent their energy on everything but study. Of the fifty, only four finished the month-long course to become part of the Corps. Mount Beulah, an old former college campus in the country near Edwards, Mississippi, had been in use by the Delta Ministry only two months; this experience set it back physically about two years.

The second group of volunteers was more carefully screened; these young people were interested, more than anything else, in freedom. Twenty strong, they worked hard at Mount Beulah; fifteen of them became members of the Corps.

Their work was a matter of pride; it certainly was no way to get rich. Their pay was the standard (then) for subsistence volunteers in the movement: ten dollars a week. Members moved, usually in pairs, into towns where the local people seemed to need help in getting organized. They went not as representatives of an organization, but as new citizens of the town working to help strengthen the existing groups.

Sam Brown and Homer Crawford went to Yazoo County, one of the meanest in the state. They were often picked up for "vagrancy" or "passing out leaflets without a permit." When they found a family who dared offer them lodging, the sheriff would visit the landlord and put on the heat to have them evicted. Still, in three months 150 black citizens registered to vote.

Joseph Harris, who later was to join the DM staff as director of the Sunflower County project, spent the first summer in Holmes County. After the special election on changing the state's voting rules, he wrote: "All of the Negroes who voted and those who attempted felt as if they had just come into their man- and womanhood because this was the first time since living in Mississippi some 21 or more years that they ever had an opportunity to exercise their right to vote. Most of them are still talking about it."

Roosevelt White, an eighteen-year-old high school senior, had been expelled (from an all-black school) because of his activities in the movement. He went to work for the Freedom Corps in his own county, Issaquena.

Weldon Davis, another eighteen-year-old, sent Curtis Hayes his monthly report with this matter-of-fact ending: "I have had little incidents: I got slapped and two of the FDP white boys got beat up and every time we go into town the police follow us around with shotguns."

Despite these working conditions, Davis reported, "I am working on school integration and we have had about 70 kids going to white schools. I am helping parents get records of vaccination papers and birth certificates; I have been using my salary to buy gas to transfer the people to the health center and back home."

Two girls, Juadine Henderson and Helen Williams, tackled some out-of-the-way towns in Bolivar County. In one, they reported, "19 students enrolled in the previously all-white school, but only 5 are now attending. The principal of the Negro high school persuaded some of the students to come back to the Negro school."

They next tried Gunnison, where "civil rights workers have been chased out of town about an hour after they arrive. The first person we contacted was a [Negro] minister. After being at his home for about 30 minutes, the sheriff rode by and saw and kept passing the house. After we left the house, the sheriff followed us until we left town. About three days later the minister who had talked so strongly for the movement came to Rosedale and suggested that we wait a while before we come back to Gunnison. We went back again and weren't noticed by anyone."

By April 1965 there were eleven people on the DM payroll, and by autumn, at least twice that. They were working in Washington, Issaquena, Sunflower, Bolivar, Hinds, and Tallahatchie counties, and only Art and Warren seemed to know what they all were doing.

I got some of the picture, vividly painted, on my first day in the office in Greenville. My wife Ginny and I had made a flying trip from Dayton, Ohio, to Greenville at Art Thomas' insistence, to see what the life was like before making a final decision about joining the staff. I had been editor of a denominational youth magazine for ten years, and the change from the cloistered life of church bureaucrat was a big one. And Art had already hired one couple who, after a couple of months in Mississippi, packed up and moved back north.

We were met at the plane by Art, a compact, intense, soft-spoken man who manages to give the impression that he knows exactly what he is doing—and most of what everybody else is doing.

Art had been in the South eleven years, getting a degree in economics at Duke, graduating from Duke's divinity school, studying more economics at its graduate school, and then organizing in Durham one of the first integrated congregations in the South. He had been adviser to a group of NAACP Youth Commandos, complete with lettered sweatshirts, long before the world was to hear of Father Groppi and the Milwaukee group of the same name. Art had gone to work for Bob Spike and the NCC's Commission on Religion and Race, eventually becoming the commission's man in Mississippi. His relationships with COFO and the black leaders of many counties were a big factor in the commission's effectiveness in the summer of 1964.

Art took us to the Greenville office—the one Warren had found after the eviction from Washington Street. This office was on Nelson, the Negro main street. A storefront sandwiched between a cafe and a beauty parlor, the office usually shook with the beat of the jukebox on the other side of the thin wall, and reeked with the acrid smell of waving lotions. There was no identifying sign in the window—just a poster like the one in the beauty parlor window:

EVERYONE
in this
ESTABLISHMENT
is a
REGISTERED VOTER
Freedom Democratic Party
and the Delta Ministry

Inside was a large room with two secretaries' desks and a conference table the size of a ping-pong table, supported by spindly legs which were always breaking down. Boxes of clothing and canned goods, sent down from the North, were piled along one wall. An old church pew, the seat cracked, was along another. Two doors led to tiny offices, partitioned off with plywood.

Ginny and I (and six-week-old Paul, who was too young to leave with a babysitter in Dayton) sat on that pew most of one day, listening to one end of dozens of phone calls and watching a stream of visitors. These were some of the signs of what we were getting into.

A hospital orderly, still in his white working clothes, rushed in to say he had just been fired for sitting down at a table on the white side of the hospital cafeteria. Warren called one of the civil rights lawyers' committees in Jackson and put the young man on the phone to them.

An old lady, bent and shaking, came in and asked for Larry Walker. We could hear enough over the partition to tell that she was being evicted, along with five children and grandchildren, from a shack in town for failing to pay the rent. She was only three days late—but that's the standard grace period for tenants in the Negro districts. Larry arranged to lend her the money until her social security came.

Bob Beech called to say that he had arranged with an Atlanta firm to rent tents for the people who were marching from Brandon, Mississippi, to Jackson in protest of conditions there. Beech, who had been lent to the Selma march and had been in charge of setting up the tents each night, during that trip, was, as a result, now the movement's tent man. A stocky, cheerful wheeler-dealer, he had been a Presbyterian pastor in Illinois before coming to Hattiesburg in spring 1964 to work with the Presbyterian Ministers' Project there. The project had become part of the Delta Ministry when the Greenville office opened in September.

The phone reported that Harry Bowie, director of the project in McComb, was in jail on some phony charge or other. (Bowie has the receipt to prove he was once arrested for "going sixty-five in a seventy-mile-an-hour zone"). Al Winham, the New England pastor who was running the Mount Beulah center near Jackson, was called and told to take bail money to McComb. Somebody kidded about Bowie "trying to get a rest."

The phone rang a few hours later to say that Al, upon arriving at the jail, had also been arrested—for something like "blocking the door of a public building" as he went into the police office. This announcement inspired more laughter and jokes, and then somebody set out for McComb to see what could be done.

Art Thomas was talking to somebody in the Department of Agriculture about surplus commodities. Armed with $30,000 made available by the National Student Association (the proceeds from a Thanksgiving "fast" on many campuses), Art had arranged with USDA for the Delta Ministry to distribute surplus food in Forrest County. Forrest was one of eighteen counties in the state which refused to give out the free food, though the need was plain, "because it cost too much—and besides, it mostly went to niggers anyway." But as soon as the county supervisors learned that DM might be given the distribution job, they quickly petitioned USDA for the chance to set up their own plan.

Art then took his plan to the next county—and to the next, and to the next—until nine counties had set up food programs reaching 64,000 people for the first time.

Warren was talking with an official of the Church of the Brethren relief agency in New Windsor, Maryland, about a plan to collect food and children's clothing in Pennsylvania, Ohio, and Kansas. The Disciples of Christ and the United Church of Christ were cooperating with the Brethren in the project.

A volunteer from Canton called in to report that fifteen sewing machines had been donated to the cooperative he was helping organize; the Madison County Sewing Firm had the promise of a contract and hoped to employ twenty-four women, he said.

Art emerged from one of the offices with a suitcase and announced he was leaving for Washington. "You have to have a job description," he said to me. "How about this?" He sat down at one of the typewriters and banged out five lines. "This will suit New York. Do you want to work for us?" Assured that we did, he waved good-bye and disappeared out the door.

Before the day was over—a day in which we adjusted somewhat reluctantly to the movement schedule of breakfast at 9:30, and lunch at 2:30—Larry had issued an invitation to me.

"I've been meeting with a group of plantation tractor drivers in the Tribbett area ever since Christmas time," he said. "They first got together to learn about voting, since many of them didn't know that Negroes could vote in the U.S.A. But lately they've been talking about a strike. Why don't you come to tonight's meeting? I can guarantee that it will be interesting."

Larry's prediction was a good one. It turned out to be the most important meeting of the Delta Ministry's young life.

# 5. The Strike That "Failed"

DICK GREGORY, Drew Pearson, and a group of church people in Vermont probably don't know to this day that they helped start the first plantation strike in the deep South in thirty years.

But the connection between them, the meeting to which Larry invited me, and the strike that spring is clear and direct.

He had first come to the Tribbett area, Larry explained before the meeting, not long before Christmas. He and other Delta Ministry staff members were delivering turkeys sent to Mississippi by the thousand by Gregory, the courageous comedian, and Pearson, the syndicated columnist. He was also delivering toys, which had filled a recently arrived medical van donated to DM by the group in Vermont.

"Everywhere I went," Larry said, "I naturally asked the

people if they were registered. It turned out that most of them did not know a Negro could vote in the United States."

Many of them said they wanted to know more. Could he hold a meeting? Sure.

But it turned out that holding a meeting was not easy in that area. "We first met in a tenant shack, owned by one of the farm hands. About twenty-five people showed up.

"The next morning the planter came around and warned the tenant that if he had any more meetings in his home, he'd be fired immediately."

The men insisted they wanted more meetings. Many of them couldn't read well enough to fill out the registration form, and they wanted to know why Larry couldn't teach them to read. And the discussion of voting had whetted their appetites for more information on how they could make things better in Mississippi.

The churches of the area seemed possible sites for a meeting, but no luck. Most of the churches were on plantation property, under control of the white planter. The pastors of the few churches which were owned by black people were afraid of nightriders or of economic pressure from whites; they said "no," too.

The place they finally found for a meeting was a shed-like room built onto the side of Roosevelt Adams' grocery, in open country two miles east of Leland. The eighty acres there was the only Negro-owned farm in the area. Mr. Adams was bitter because a member of his family had been tortured by nightriders, and he gladly offered the room.

Euphemistically called a cafe, the room has a jukebox, two or three tables, a few rickety chairs and a sagging floor you can look down through. It is no more than ten by twenty feet, but seventy-five men crowded into it the first night of meetings.

All during the winter they came, two nights a week, to learn about voting, about citizenship, about their rights, about individual pride, about Negro history. Often they talked late into the night.

As the weeks went on, the plantation hands grew more confident and began to assume more of the leadership.

One young man whose voice began to be heard was Isaac Foster. A handsome, broad-shouldered guy who had grown up in the area but who had drifted around the country—doing such things as hustling pool and working a stint at the Greenville Mill, he said—Isaac was a powerful speaker. He had finished school and planned to go on to college, but he knew and understood the problems of the others.

Isaac had a special reason to want a new Mississippi. His grandfather had been a landowner, but had made the mistake of granting shelter to a traveling white man one night in the 1920s. "The man just stayed on and stayed on," Isaac says, "and finally it was my grandfather who moved out."

Isaac's father had been a landowner, too. "We heard rumors they were trying to get somebody to kill my father," he says, "because he was planning to buy more land. Several times we found people prowling around our house at night.

"Then one day, while my father was in the house and the rest of us were working in the cotton not far away, we heard a shot. I ran to the house, and almost ran into a man coming out the front door. He ran away down the road.

"Inside I found my father with his head blown off. The shotgun that did it was in another room. A few minutes later, while we were standing around thinking what to do, the sheriff came tearing up in his truck. We didn't have a phone, and hadn't called anybody. But the sheriff came in and said, 'I hear Willie Foster's committed suicide.'

"That's what the verdict was, too—suicide."

Another emerging leader was John Henry Sylvester, who was living proof that you didn't have to have an education to have brains or leadership ability. Mr. Sylvester couldn't write much more than his own name, but he knew what the world was about, and he knew about people. A skilled welder and carpenter, he was shop foreman on the A. L. Andrews plantation, where he drew the same six dollars a day pay that the tractor drivers did.

The meetings in Roosevelt Adams' store branched out from voting and literacy to include working conditions. Isaac Foster had visited Shaw, where black people were forming a Mississippi Freedom Labor Union among tractor drivers and maids. He suggested that the men of the Tribbett area ought to band together and demand better wages from the big three planters, Walker, Dean, and Andrews. After weeks of palavering, stretching into the spring planting season, the men began to talk strike.

The night Larry invited me to the meeting at the store was hot and muggy, with the stink of the "poison," as the field hands called the weed-killing sprays, hovering over the cotton. At least sixty men had crowded into the tiny room, making the heat almost unbearable to somebody who wasn't used to Mississippi summers.

But the room was full of excitement. The men sang a few songs like "Ain't Gonna Let Nobody Turn Me 'Round" and "Oh Freedom," and Isaac and John Henry and Larry Walker made speeches. But it was obvious that no urging was necessary. The men had talked strike; the spies in their midst had reported to the planters, who made threats; now it was time to act. When Isaac called for the vote, every man raised his hand and shouted "aye" at the same time. The men, representing most of the skilled work force on the three major plantations, agreed they would refuse to work on the following Monday unless they got some kind of raise. Their goal was $1.25 an hour, the minimum wage.

That was on Thursday night. On the following Monday morning, Mr. Wallace Greene, the timekeeper on the Andrews plantation, approached Mr. Andrews in the driveway at the plantation center. Behind him were the eleven other men classified as tractor drivers on the farm. Behind Mr. Andrews was his attorney and a deputy sheriff; he'd already had a full report on the meeting in the store.

"We ask you once more, Mr. Andrews, if we can have a raise," Mr. Greene said.

"Hell, no," Andrews replied, "I've told you no. Before I'd go up, I'd go down. You work for what I pay you, or get out."

Silently, Wallace Greene handed over the timekeeper's watch, symbol of his job, and turned with the other men to go back to their homes. It was the end of seven and a half years on the plantation for Mr. Greene.

Within twenty-four hours, deputy sheriffs had arrived and, with the help of trustees from the Washington County jail, took every stick of furniture from the tenant houses and stacked it in the ditch alongside the road.

The next afternoon, in the Delta Ministry office in Greenville, the men learned that workers on the other two plantations had backed down. The owners, although they had earlier agreed with Andrews not to raise wages, had granted an increase to seven dollars a day and promised to fix up the tenant shacks.

The strikers learned, too, what happens to men who dare to threaten the economy of a whole county. They had been unable to find anybody in Greenville, black or

Wallace Greene, former timekeeper and field boss on the Andrews plantation, with granddaughter Helen (*Bruce Hilton*)

white, who dared rent one of them a place to live—although there were dozens of empty rental houses in town.

Some of them had been out job-hunting, and already had learned from one frank white man that "there never will be jobs for you men anywhere in this county, ever again."

The blacklisting was to last more than a year. I remember once in September three of the strikers bursting into the Greenville office to report that they had been hired at a cotton gin in town—and then fired twenty minutes later when the owner discovered who they were. The only job offers any of them got were in widely scattered towns outside Mississippi—and were obviously designed to break up the group and get the men out of the Delta. They refused to go. "We come together this far, we'll stick together."

The Delta Ministry staff found transportation for the wives and children of the Andrews plantation to go to Mount Beulah, the newly opened conference center a hundred miles south near Edwards. The men pitched a tent in the shade of Roosevelt Adams' store and slept there.

During the daylight hours, they picketed the Andrews plantation. This wasn't easy, since it consisted of more than a thousand acres and was reached by several roads.

But each morning, before dawn, the men would deploy to the various entrances to intercept the choppers' buses. Each day they would get the driver to stop and let one of them climb aboard the bus. There the strikers would plead with the people who were paying fifty cents apiece to the bus driver to bring them out from town, "Please don't work on this plantation. We're on strike."

Sometimes it was stronger than pleading. Black people

Strike City, January 1966 (*Bruce Hilton*)

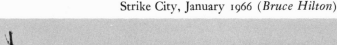

in Greenville began phoning the black owners of buses who tried to carry people out to the Andrews place, and when persuasion didn't work, they used some threats.

Press coverage of the strike concentrated on Larry Walker—possibly because of the feeling that only a white man could conceive such a program. One story earned Larry the undying hatred of Delta whites by describing him as "loping" across the fields in a pith helmet which he said he wore "because it bugs the rednecks."

The number of drivers willing to deliver workers to the Andrews place got fewer and fewer. And of those busloads which did go, only one all summer voted to go on into the plantation after hearing the strikers' plea.

Andrews filed an injunction, limiting the pickets to four and forbidding any employee of the Delta Ministry to set foot on the Walker, Dean, or Andrews plantations. Andrews imported poor white workers from Arkansas after failing to find a single black tractor driver who would move in; he renovated the tenant shacks but insisted he wasn't paying higher wages. Andrews charged that Dave DiRienzis, a Delta Ministry volunteer, had slapped a Negro worker who was hauling workers to the plantation in a station wagon; an accommodating judge sentenced Dave to six months in jail. Dave and his bride of three weeks left the state and the Delta Ministry.

Late in the summer, DM helped the men, who now called themselves Mississippi Freedom Labor Union, Local Number Four, buy eight big army tents and five acres of land next to the Adams store. The families were brought back from Mount Beulah and installed in the tents. A sign near the road, occasionally punctuated with buckshot, bore the union name, a clenched fist breaking a chain, and the name "Strike City."

The families would live in the tents, through hot summer and bitter winter, for a year and three weeks. In December, twenty-five students from the University of Pennsylvania came down, armed with blueprints, enthusiasm and $6000 in cash, and with the help and guidance of the strikers, built a community center at Strike City.

Delta Ministry put on a national campaign for funds, raising enough to keep the families eating and clothed through the winter.

In the spring, an anonymous Chicago resident who had seen the publicity—including two long sequences on the Walter Cronkite news show at Christmas time—sent $40,-000 to help build permanent homes.

*Look* magazine also sent a writer-camera crew, doing a sensitive picture story entitled "The Strike That Failed." Their headline agreed with the estimate of many strangers who heard the Strike City story. But not with that of the strikers themselves, nor of the residents of the Tribbett area.

Today, cars with white passengers and cars with black passengers still drive down old U.S. 80 east of Leland to take a look at the neat, white, two-story houses with the sign "Strike City" in front. To the whites, the fact that twelve men had the guts to ask for a fair day's wage, and to stick together in their defiance of pressure, is a disturbing—and educating—fact. To the black people, the fact that men could stand up to the white planter, and not only get away with it but gain support from all across the country for their stand, is a promise and a challenge.

There were few other strikers in the Delta that year or since. The strike actually helped hasten mechanization and the use of weed killers, and thus the exodus from the Delta.

But there are few black people in all the Delta who will agree that it was a strike that failed.

# 6. Long Cold Winter

"Nobody is starving in Mississippi. The nigra women I see are so fat they shine."—Governor Paul Johnson, TV INTERVIEW, April 13, 1967

IN THREE HECTIC MONTHS, from November 1965 to February 1966, the Delta Ministry made a drastic change in program, took on a new group of refugees, made national headlines—and very nearly went down the drain.

For the poor people in the Delta, it was the worst winter in years. The temperature got as low as five degrees, with bitter winds and more snow than usual. Worse, for many of the plantation tenants there was this winter no "furnish" —the food money usually advanced by the plantation owner, and repaid from spring wages. Planters were telling tenants by the thousands that there would be no work in the spring.

Gene Roberts, the able *New York Times* correspondent working out of Atlanta, quoted Ralph Alewine of the Mississippi Employment Service on November 18, 1965, as saying that 6,500 tractor drivers would be out of work next spring. Figuring conservatively, this meant 35,000 people without any income and, eventually, without homes.

Most of the planters told their extra workers they could stay on in the shacks, at least through the winter. But many of the planters felt they could no longer advance money for the light bill, since the tenant would have no way to repay it.

There was a double reason for the decrease in jobs. First, the mechanization of cotton picking and the development of weed killers (under federal sponsorship) had for some years been reducing the need for hand labor. The percentage of the Mississippi crop picked by machine rose from 42 to 62 percent between 1960 and 1964; by 1968 it would be 85 percent. Late in 1965, the long-promised pre-emergent weed killers—which could be sprayed on fields by airplane before the cotton stalks came up—were perfected and on the market. These liquids, whose sour smell

Winstonville, all-Negro town of five hundred, where only a dozen men have jobs (*Bruce Hilton*)

hung over the Delta in the spring and could be detected not only in the heart of town but in an airliner three thousand feet above the ground, eliminated at once most of the part-time "chopping" with which the Delta's old folks and children stretched family incomes. And since they eliminated half the reason for maintaining tenant families on the farm, they made many planters decide the cost of such maintenance—even at three to six dollars a day—was too high.

The second and more catastrophic reason for job decreases was Congress' new program for cutting back on cotton growing. Your congressman and mine approved a bill which offered incentives to the planters to cut back their cotton acreage by as much as 35 percent. The planters lost little, if any, income. But Congress failed to show the same concern for the tenants, mostly black people, who worked the fields. Many of them lost everything.

Vernon Dahmer's ranch home the day after the White Knights burned it and killed him (*Bruce Hilton*)

The effect of Congress' one-sided concern could be seen in a place like Winstonville, an all-Negro town of about five hundred people. It had been built by white planters in a day when it was essential to have a pool of Negro laborers nearby, ready to work the fields when the weather was good. In recent years, the part-time chopping in spring and picking in the fall had been the main source of income. Only thirteen men in town had regular jobs, mostly in factories in Cleveland; the one store in town did a gross business of $200 a week, or about forty cents worth of food per person.

When the chopping and picking jobs disappeared, even that meager economic base disappeared.

My wife, Ginny, a registered nurse, drove the eighty-mile round trip to Winstonville each Wednesday to conduct mothers' classes in hygiene and nutrition, and to help local people organize a "freedom school" for children whose regular school experience was pretty rigid and conformist. She found an air of quiet desperation; many people were living solely on government surplus commodities designed to supplement diets, and had no idea what they would do in the spring when the commodities stopped coming.

These commodities, meanwhile, were at the heart of a battle the Delta Ministry was fighting with the capitols in Washington and Jackson. It involved a state-wide distribution plan called Operation Help, which the Department of Agriculture and the state of Mississippi had cooked up after DM had bluffed nine counties into starting distribution of commodities.

The intent of the plan, as far as Mississippi was concerned, was to keep the Delta Ministry from distributing U.S. government food to the poor in *any* county. This was fine with DM, which didn't have the money to handle such a program anyway; it just wanted people to get the food.

But negotiations had been dragging on for nearly a year. The Agriculture Department wrote DM several times in the fall promising action soon and reporting that both USDA and the state estimated that an additional 500,000 people not then receiving commodities ought to be doing so—making a total of 800,000, or a third of the state's population.

The government wanted promises from the state that it would appoint a biracial board to administer the program and that nearly five hundred people would be hired, without racial discrimination, to work in the warehouses. The state's failure to do these things was what was delaying the program.

A delegation of poor Negroes called upon Miss Evelyn Gandy, the red-haired professional politician who ran the state welfare program. A former assistant to the famous racist Senator Theodore Bilbo, Miss Gandy received the delegation cordially, but in the words of one member, "said as little as she could get away with." It became obvious that she had little enthusiasm for Operation Help—especially for its hiring of poor black people.

On November 23, though, state officials signed a contract for the project, and agreed to implement it within sixty days.

The state's black citizens, increasingly aware of how their lives were affected by state and federal officials, were also angry over the failure of OEO to refund the Child Development Group of Mississippi.

This Head Start program, the largest in the country, had been organized in the state despite the governor's veto, thanks to a loophole allowing an obscure nonprofit institution, Mary Holmes Junior College, to act as grantee in such cases. The only people who would have anything to do with it at first were movement people, and various movement groups had helped get it going. DM's role had been to help organize the sixty or so local committees which ran the schools, a job the staff and ten volunteers accomplished in a little over two weeks.

CDGM's headquarters was at Mount Beulah, and the program's popularity with Governor Johnson is indicated by the fact that the headquarters staff collected $1100 in traffic fines its first week, just driving out the Mount Beulah gate!

Senator Stennis, with spectacular public charges of mismanagement and fraud, and with quiet but firm use of political clout in the cloakrooms, had managed to keep Sargent Shriver from continuing the program beyond September, when its first grant ran out. Highly praised by educators as effective education, and by OEO officials as the country's best showpiece of "maximum feasible participation by the poor," CDGM had brought thirteen hundred jobs to poor adults, mostly black, and was helping six thousand children. Now it was being held up, and the people were angry.

This was the situation on New Year's Day 1966—the start of the most crucial month in the Delta Ministry's life. Here's a log of some of the events of that month.

*January 4.* Fifty crosses are burned by the Klan in Mississippi, signaling an end to the "moratorium on violence" reportedly requested by state leaders in the fall and early winter.

*January 6.* The Freedom Democratic Party announces it will enter candidates in the fall congressional elections for the first time. Candidates include Lawrence Guyot, chairman of the FDP, and three Methodist ministers.

*January 8.* The Freedom Information Service reports:

"Over 2,200 people have moved off their plantation homes in six Delta counties since last August." In Ruleville, FIS says, eight families were evicted from one plantation, including Mrs. Sallie Mae Carthen, an FDP worker whose husband is in the hospital.

*January 10.* Vernon Dahmer is killed by nightriders. A long-time friend of the Delta Ministry, he had supported the state's first two voter-registration workers in 1960.

He had been awakened around 2 A.M. by gunfire outside his isolated farm home, a few miles from Hattiesburg. As he ran toward the front room, there was a crash of glass and three plastic bottles filled with gasoline exploded in flame.

The fire spread quickly, and Dahmer could see his small store, twenty yards away, also in flames. He roused his wife, two sons, and a daughter, but as they tried to escape they found that the doors were splintering under a steady hail of bullets. Dahmer, with two guns, stood in the flames at the front window, firing back while the rest of the family jumped out back windows.

He died that afternoon (in the Negro wing of a segregated hospital still receiving federal funds) of burns in his lungs incurred while he covered his family's escape.

In the front row at his funeral were his four oldest sons, all in the uniform of the U.S. Army. The government had flown them back from bases in Germany, Alaska, and the United States.

Mr. Dahmer had done with his life exactly what black people are always being exhorted to do: worked hard, saved his money, turned thrift and sweat into a cotton farm, a sawmill, and a grocery. His fight for justice had always been through the quiet, legal methods. He had made some old school buildings on his land available for some DM projects and a Head Start school, and the event which triggered the murder was an announcement that Negroes who were hesitant to go into the Forrest County Courthouse to register could come instead to Dahmer's grocery.

*January 14.* A private school, the Tunica Institute of Learning, opens in the Tunica Methodist Church. The forty-three students qualify for $92.50 per semester tuition from the state. Approximately one thousand Mississippi children are now registered in such segregated schools —many of them in churches.

The same day sees a debate in the state legislature over a bill to divide the Delta congressional district, with its two-thirds black population, into three pieces and connect each piece with a predominantly white district. (The bill eventually passed.)

*January 15.* The Lee County welfare agent announces that he favors Operation Help, since it will cut down the six-month waiting period now necessary for getting on the commodities list.

*January 20.* The Clarke County welfare agent tells a delegation of black people that she doesn't know anything about Operation Help. Then she admits she does know, but doesn't intend to hire any Negroes.

*January 21.* The committee set up by the National Council of Churches to evaluate the Delta Ministry holds its first meeting in New York. Though enemies of DM hope to use the committee to discredit the project, word comes to Art Thomas that if he can avoid large, unusual expenditures and widely publicized confrontations for a little while, the chances of survival are good.

*January 22.* It snows for the third time in a week. The temperature goes down to eighteen degrees.

*January 24.* The deadline for the promised start of Operation Help. No sign of the food. Staffs of the Delta Ministry, the Freedom Democratic Party, and the Mississippi Freedom Labor Union hold a day-long meeting in Greenville; they agree to call a "Poor Peoples Conference," asking as many people as possible from all over the state to come to Mount Beulah to discuss what to do about the commodities, about CDGM, and about jobs and housing.

*January 25.* Plans are made for recruiting and transporting as many people as possible to Mount Beulah.

*January 27.* The *Democrat-Times* reports that Mrs. Pearly Williams, sixty-two, was found dead in her tenant shack near Estill, and that Jebb Willis, eighty, was found dead about half a mile from his shack on the Law plantation near Chatham. Sheriff's deputies investigated, the paper says, and "concluded that both Mrs. Williams and Willis had frozen to death."

*January 29.* The Poor Peoples Conference opens at Mount Beulah.

The thirty-five-acre campus with its thirteen buildings has seen some hectic and confused meetings since the Delta Ministry took a lease there in March 1965, and this is one of the biggest. Built by the Disciples of Christ and operated for many years as a high school and junior college for Negroes (under the name Southern Christian Institute) the campus had been used only for an occasional summer camp since SCI merged with Tougaloo College twelve years earlier.

Since March, however, Beulah had housed two contingents of Freedom Corps trainees, a state FDP convention, the evicted plantation strikers from Tribbett, meetings of CORE, SCLC, the Episcopal Society for Cultural and Racial Unity, the Poor Peoples Corporation (a co-op project, not to be confused with the Poor Peoples Conference), and the Freedom Now Brick Factory, Inc. Demonstrations and mass arrests at the state capitol had brought hundreds of volunteers from the rest of the state in June 1965; they used Mount Beulah as a staging area. The headquarters building was a big, white, 1840 plantation house, from whose porch slaves had once been sold.

More than seven hundred people are at Beulah sometimes over the weekend. Feeding and housing them, in facilities designed for about two hundred, is one of the more hectic activities. Many families have brought what belongings they can carry, with no intention of going back to the plantation. "I was afraid my baby would freeze to death," one mother confided. "There was snow on his quilt this morning."

In true movement, tradition, everybody is encouraged to speak. There is much singing of spirituals and freedom songs, much praying, and an increasingly militant tone in the speeches. Those who want to speak form two lines, one at each side of the stage in Till Hall. Someone from the line at the left makes a speech, and then someone from the right. The auditorium holds a continually changing capacity crowd of about 250.

Proposals range from a march on Jackson to guerrilla warfare. As discussion continues, resentment is aimed more and more at the federal, rather than at the state, government. "What do you expect from Mississippi?" one speaker says. "Nothin'! But the federal government ought to know better."

In the afternoon, the conference sends a telegram to President Johnson, telling him of the need for jobs and decent houses and asking his help.

*January 30.* There is no answer from the President. Various speakers suggest camping on federal land to dramatize the demand for jobs. At the request of the conference, two young white girl volunteers "case" the Yazoo National Wildlife Refuge, halfway between Mount Beulah and Greenville, as a possible demonstration spot. The superintendent is flattered at the interest shown in his facilities by the two pretty girls.

Delegates who have transistor radios hear on news broadcasts that the FBI is "pushing its search for the murderers of civil rights leader Vernon Dahmer," and that jukebox dealer Sam Bowers will testify in the HUAC investigation of the Klan the next day in Washington. (Bowers was later indicted for planning Dahmer's death.)

Some of the speakers at the conference call for burning down the warehouses where the commodities are stored. Some call for building their own town on public land. But increasingly, people seem to favor the idea of going to the Greenville Air Force Base—a complex of three hundred carefully preserved buildings, most of which have been empty since the air force closed its pilot training program there in 1960. (Although the speeches at the conference were taped, it is impossible to reproduce them because the tapes disappeared the day the conference closed. A year later, a Methodist district superintendent interrupted a heated phone discussion with me to say, "Don't tell me about that conference. The chief of police showed me a transcript of every word spoken there.")

There is some hesitation among the delegates about going onto the air base because trespassing on federal land is something new in the civil rights struggle; going to the federal pen in Atlanta is different from a stretch, no matter how vicious, in Parchman penitentiary.

It is Isaac Foster, late Sunday afternoon, who finally says, "All right. All you who want to go home, go home. All you who want to stay here, stay here. Anybody who wants to go to the air base with me, let's go, because I'm going."

With him in the caravan making the one-hundred-mile trip to Greenville that night were people from Rosedale,

Jackson, Winstonville, Natchez, Hattiesburg, Tahola, Columbus, Greenwood, and a dozen other towns. There were people who had never been more than five miles from their home plantation before, and a scattering of civil rights workers. Two of the men of Strike City were in the caravan, and a reporter from Copenhagen, Denmark.

And there were seven Delta Ministry staff members or volunteers. Having encouraged the poor people to make their own decision about their own needs, the staff felt it must abide by the decision. Art Thomas and six others were along as the group arrived at the Herbert Lee Center in Greenville to spend the night; the rest of the staff would stand by outside the air base to provide logistical support —or money for bail.

# 7. The Day They Took the Air Base

"Whenever a people are impious enough to abolish institutions founded in wisdom and compatible to justice and the indispensable necessities of the constitution, it becomes [our] duty . . . to enforce obedience, by whatever means wisdom and justice shall direct."—London MORNING POST, August 20, 1776, in answer to the Declaration by the American colonials

"SOME OF US SLEPT and some of us were too afraid to sleep the night before we went into the air force base," Isaac Foster recalls.

"Some of the folks tried to keep their afraidness from taking possession of them by staying up and talking and telling themselves that they weren't afraid."

The people in the Herbert Lee Center that night weren't people who frightened easily. But there was reason for being afraid. "In the morning," Isaac continues, "we held a meeting and I said, 'Do you realize that we are breaking into federal government property and that this could be a federal crime?"

When he was done speaking, there were forty-one who still wanted to go.

As the meeting turned to planning, somebody put the blankets and what was left of the food into the cars. The group decided the cars would stay close together, going through the airbase gate, so that they could roll as one unit and keep moving if the guard tried to stop them.

They elected Isaac Foster, Mrs. Unita Blackwell of the FDP in Issaquena County, and Mrs. Ida Mae Lawrence of the Freedom Labor Union in Bolivar County as their spokesmen. These three and no others, would talk to the press or to government officials.

Then they piled into the cars parked across the road. The caravan moved west on Belle Air to Broadway, and then north on the four-lane road to the air base. There were still patches of ice on the concrete.

"The man at the gate just smiled and waved his hand," Isaac Foster recalls.

"And then suddenly he realized there were a line of cars full of people dressed like they were going to the cotton fields with babies in their arms. He tried to stop the cars, but it was too late."

The building toward which the cars turned was T-shaped, a big, gray, wooden barracks. The caravan halted at one end of the T's crossbar and everybody piled out. One of the men from the first car pried loose the hasp holding the padlock on the building's main door. Lugging blankets and boxes of food, the group filed around the end of a reception counter and into a room which made up one of the arms of the T. It wasn't much warmer inside; they curled up in the blankets and waited to see what would happen.

Foster Davis, managing editor of the local newspaper, remembers that it was a typical Monday morning on the

*Democrat-Times*—"calling around the beats, and trying to catch up on the wrecks and stabbings over the weekend."

Around eight o'clock, Davis got a call from a Boston newspaper. "They had heard from a woman in Boston whose husband was supposed to be in a demonstration at the Greenville Air Force Base," he says.

"I nearly dropped the phone, but I said, 'Hold on, we're checking it out now.'

"I called the base and asked Colonel Andrew. He admitted that 'Yes, indeed, we do have a situation out here.'

"I said, 'Thank you,' hung up the phone, and got on out there!"

Others were on their way out there, too. Not sure about who had jurisdiction, Colonel Andrew had called both the Greenville police and the Washington County sheriff. The county attorney arrived, and soon afterward the local FBI agent. The correspondent for the *Commercial Appeal* and the local UPI stringer also came driving up.

In the confusion one reporter was allowed in to interview the demonstrators, while others were stopped; they were told that if they entered the building they would be guilty of trespassing!

Lieutenant Colonel Andrew, whose predecessor as base commander had privately admitted a lingering fear that civil rights demonstrators would someday come to the base, went inside the building to address the demonstrators. You are trespassing on government property," he said. "You must all leave now."

Mrs. Lawrence handed him a crudely mimeographed sheet, run off at Mount Beulah the night before, listing the Poor Peoples' demands: food, jobs, job training or an income, land, an end to Operation HELP under control of county supervisors, and the refunding of Head Start.

Colonel Andrew's response was, "My only concern is

with this building." He locked the doors to all the other rooms in the building. Stumbling over the feet of one of the trespassers, Andrew accused him of kicking him in the shin.

News coverage of this incident was indicative of what was to come. *The New York Times* quoted the commander as saying he had been kicked, but carefully added that Colonel Andrew later changed his mind and "said he did not know if the bumping or kicking was intentional." In contrast, Ed Moore of the *Commercial Appeal* huffed, "An Air Force lieutenant colonel who tried to reason with the whites and Negroes received a kick in the shin from one of them for his trouble. The officer is a Korean war hero."

Soon after Colonel Andrew left, the people put up a hand-lettered sign on the outside door: "This is our home. Please knock before entering."

Most of the action between 8 A.M. and noon was on the telephone. Andrew, whose total military force was twenty-eight enlisted men, had talked with his superior, Major General R. W. Puryear of Keesler Air Force Base in Biloxi. He had also been in touch with the air force chief of staff, the United States attorney at Oxford, the Justice Department in Washington, and an aide at the White House.

Around ten o'clock a technician began installing extra telephones in the command post.

Back in Greenville, both phones in the Delta Ministry office were busy, too. The movement was preparing to back up the first wave of demonstrators with food, clothes, and more people. One staffer was soliciting local Negroes for meals that could be brought into the base hot; another was trying to keep some record of the people who soon would be joining the demonstrators.

Five of the young men and women of the Freedom Corps were back out on the plantations, where they had spent the previous two weeks; they were spreading the word that if families faced eviction, they could join the demonstrators at the air base.

One call that got through to the DM office was from the little store at Strike City; Mrs. John Henry Sylvester reported that the families there would be responsible for feeding the demonstrators. And if the people were evicted, they could set up tents at Strike City, she said.

Another call was from the Civil Rights Commission in Washington. An administrative assistant was demanding to know why the people had occupied the base. Warren McKenna told him about the general condition of people in the Delta, the cold, and the fact that two people had frozen to death on Wednesday. "We can't deal with the general condition," the CRC man sputtered. "Besides, there is no excuse for breaking the law." Warren told him he'd have to tell it to the people in the barracks.

The DM office was filling up with people—many of them from the conference at Beulah, the rest rounded up by the Freedom Corps or notified by the movement grapevine. Though they were ready to go into the base, most of them were instead put to work planning, organizing, cutting stencils, making phone calls, soliciting food, and generally becoming a logistics support team for the people in the barracks.

A little before noon, a second group of demonstrators had been chosen and drove off in four cars toward the cold and hungry people at the base.

While the police, the sheriff's deputies, the FBI, and the air force men watched in surprise, they came skidding through the gate. No one had thought to bar it.

They parked beside the barracks and unloaded mattresses, more blankets, cartons of food, and two small wood-burning stoves.

Fifteen people had come in the second wave, including a

large family from a Sunflower County plantation. But the most welcome sight was the food and stoves. The demonstrators knocked out two small window panes and stuck the stove pipes out through the holes. Quickly they cooked and began to enjoy their first hot food of the day.

They also began to organize for a long stay. After a long, rambling discussion they chose committees to keep the room clean, to prepare food, and to tend the stoves. They reaffirmed their choice of three spokesmen, and talked about what to do if evicted. It was agreed, and emphasized again by Isaac Foster, that there must be no violence. "If you're not planning to be nonviolent then you should go out now," he said, "because no matter how you might feel about it, you will just destroy what we're trying to do here."

They were a widely assorted crew. There was Mrs. Viola Wall, who had come to Mount Beulah because she was afraid she would freeze to death in her shack. She had

Inside the "captured" building at the air base: Art Thomas (with cigarette in hand), Nash Basom, Isaac Foster, Unita Blackwell (*Mary Varela*)

survived the winter so far only "by cutting and selling fire-wood like a man," she said.

Mrs. Lula Mae Brooks, who fifteen months later would be a candidate for city council in Sunflower, was there. Veterans of many a demonstration were also there, like Johnnie Mae Walker of Hattiesburg and Ida Mae Lawrence of Rosedale. So were whole families who had never been "with the civil rights" before.

The first group had been forty Negroes and ten whites. Most of the latter were civil rights workers—"COFO left-overs" or DM staff and volunteers—but one was a reporter from Copenhagen, Denmark, who seemed to have lost his journalistic cool.

The new arrivals brought word of what might be a problem—the arrival in Greenville of an increasing number of "boppers." These were the walking wounded of the freedom movement—teenagers, mostly, but some college dropouts too. The majority were native Negro Mississippians who had been caught up in the excitement of the 1964 summer, and were left at loose ends when COFO broke up at the end of that year. Some were whites who had never gone home after that summer. Most of them lived without visible means of support, moving from home to home whenever they could find a bed. They always showed up when there was action, somehow managing to find transportation, no matter where they had been when they got the word.

Many of them had been at the Mount Beulah conference. The demonstrators inside the air base knew them and liked most of them. But this was supposed to be a demonstration by poor people, not by civil rights workers. And they knew from experience that the boppers, many of them made cynical by the exodus of the big civil rights groups, or shell-shocked from too much tension over too long a time, weren't very reliable. The boppers rejected tight group discipline, which was part of planned civil disobedience.

So the word went out from the barracks, "Send us the evicted families, but tell the civil rights workers and boppers to stay where they are. They can serve best by supplying us, and by spreading the word to other homeless families that here is a place to live."

While it was warming up in the barracks, it was turning colder outside. The wind was getting stronger. The air force was now stopping every car that tried to pass through the gate, carefully quizzing the driver—who was usually going to meet a plane.

Around noon, Chief Burnley of the Greenville police decided to take his men back to town. The discussion about jurisdiction had gone on all morning; Greenville is painfully sensitive about its national image, and neither Burnley nor Chief Deputy Earl Fisher wanted to play the villain when the eviction came.

Nobody was sure just who was responsible for the air base. The air force had already announced plans to turn some of the buildings over to the state and the rest to the city sometime soon. But as of now, the federal government probably owned the barrack in question.

The city of Greenville, however, had never relinquished title to the *land* on which the base was built. One of the law enforcement men told a reporter mournfully, "It is a case of breaking and entering on what may be city property or what might be a federal reservation in what we *know* is Washington County, Mississippi."

The county attorney told the chief, the chief deputy, and the unhappy base commander that, in his opinion, the responsibility belonged strictly to the air force. As Burnley rounded up his policemen, a reporter asked him if he were pulling out. "You're damn right!" he said. He and his men drove off shortly thereafter.

Their departure didn't make much of a dent in the growing crowd, however. By now a CBS-TV news team had arrived in a chartered Lear jet. A fire truck and crew had been summoned from the other side of the air base, to stand nervous watch on the smoke coming from the two stovepipes. Greenville radios were interrupting their regular broadcasts every ten or fifteen minutes to report the break-in, and Greenvillians were driving out to watch.

The Justice Department was now on hand, in the person of a young man who had just been transferred from the peace and quiet of the tax division. He had been on his way to Mississippi to check on school desegregation in Issaquena County, but was diverted to the air base instead. He looked uncomfortable. "I asked him whether the people in the barrack would be prosecuted," newsman Foster Davis recalls. "He just kind of looked at me like, 'Gosh, I wish you hadn't asked me that.'"

Reporters, eager for action, were pressing Colonel Andrew about his plans. At three in the afternoon he still had to tell them, "I don't expect to make a move at any time in the immediate future."

Andrew had been in touch with Attorney General Katzenbach, who had been in emergency session with Sargent Shriver and Agriculture Secretary Orville Freeman. Washington, always so sensitive to the feelings of Mississippi congressmen, was now feeling pressure from another direction: officials feared the reaction that might follow an eviction of homeless people from an otherwise unoccupied building.

Colonel Andrew had also been talking frequently to General Puryear, and had word that the general was on his way to Greenville.

Inside the barracks, the demonstrators were enjoying the knowledge that they finally had caught the attention of the folks in Washington. The young Justice Department man was one of the visitors. He surveyed the scene—the potbellied stoves, the cans of food stacked along the walls, people dozing on the floor, plantation women dressed in trousers made of old blankets, babies crying. "Who's in charge here?" he finally asked.

"We don't have no leaders," Isaac Foster told him, "but I will speak to you."

"Can't I talk to you alone?" the lawyer asked.

"We're all here together, and you can talk to all of us," Ike said. "This is our house, and we ain't ashamed to talk in our house."

The lawyer lowered his voice. "You have violated federal law, you know. But we have decided to let you go. If you leave right away, that is."

Ike sighed, "Mister, you don't seem to understand. Most of these people don't have any place to go."

Half an hour later, Ike says, another lawyer came in. The air force had a plane waiting, the man told him, to fly the leaders of the Poor Peoples' Conference to Washington to meet with Freeman, Shriver, and Katzenbach.

Ike, who had been a delegate to a White House conference on civil rights, was not impressed. "Let them fly here," he said, "and see what things are like in the Delta."

There were no more official visitors that afternoon. But more people and more supplies were arriving. Despite the guard at the front gate, whole families were finding their way onto the base and into the barrack.

At 7:30 P.M. a support group successfully smuggled a hot spaghetti dinner for sixty-five people over the back fence of the base.

Between supper and midnight, twenty-five more people

joined the group, bringing food, medicine, portable radios, and firewood.

Beginning around midnight, and at frequent intervals afterward, those who were awake heard large planes circling low over the base. "Thank the Lord," one mother, who had come to the base from a plantation, told her two children, "President Johnson is sending food for the folks in the Delta."

But the planes weren't bringing food. After eighteen months of inaction in the Delta, the federal government was demonstrating that it could act when it wanted to.

The planes, rendezvousing from five air bases as far away as Denver, were carrying troops. More than 150 air policemen, two full colonels, three lieutenant colonels, three majors, and a major general were being flown in to evict the people from the building.

The demonstrators awoke on Tuesday morning to see that the clouds were gone; it was a bright, brisk, clear day. The stove committee began stoking the fires, and the cleanup committee rolled up the mattresses and folded blankets.

They could look out the windows to see a crowd even bigger than yesterday's clustered around the entrance to the base. There were TV camera crews from all three national networks, plus photographers from the wire services and half a dozen newspapers. There seemed to be more of the anonymous-looking men in conservative business suits who showed up at every demonstration, representing one government agency or another.

The crowd inside had grown, too. New residents had come over, around, and under the base fence, until there were about one hundred people in the room. Isaac Foster,

Mrs. Blackwell, and Mrs. Lawrence called a meeting after breakfast to discuss plans for the day.

At the Delta Ministry office in Greenville, movement people allied with the Freedom Democratic Party, the Freedom Labor Union, the Vermont in Mississippi project, and the Freedom Information Service, and all the other groups left in the state were working as a team. The emphasis had changed overnight, however, from recruiting people to finding land. It was obvious that the demonstrators would be evicted; they needed a place to go. Staff members, volunteers, and boppers called their "contacts" in the North, seeking money for land; the Mississippians were calling Negro landowners as far away as Memphis to find what was available. When somebody laid down a phone for a moment, it would ring—often with a voice from some government office in Washington, asking why DM hadn't told them about conditions in the Delta before.

The troops who had arrived the night before were housed in a pair of big empty hangars along the flight line. Experienced air policemen, they were taken in groups of thirty-five to a classroom building for briefing. "You will probably be spit upon and cursed," they were told by a colonel from Texas, "but handle these people gently. The eyes of the country are on you."

After the briefings, the men went back to the hangars to wait. Some slept, some played poker for nickels and dimes on a GI blanket. The officers were clustered in and around the command post, where General Puryear was still trying to get decisions from the various federal agencies he had called.

At eleven that morning, the troops were called together and formed into ranks. Dressed in fatigues and carrying billy clubs, they marched down the broad center street of the base, past row on row of empty barracks, past the unused chapel, around the empty flag pole to the gate. They halted outside the demonstrators' barrack and came to parade rest. Then General Puryear went inside.

The TV cameras and the reporters went in, too. The general fidgeted, while technicians set up lights and microphones and reporters found places to stand along the walls.

"Now you people have violated the federal law by coming in here," the general began. "More important, you have become a source of danger to government property, and, I might add, to yourselves.

"My first responsibility is to this building. But I am also concerned about you. You must realize that without running water or sanitation facilities this building is both a fire and health hazard. I must ask you again to leave."

"Shoot, man," Isaac Foster interrupted, "don't you know that ninety percent of the Negro houses in Mississippi don't have running water or inside toilets? We feel right at home here—and a whole lot warmer!"

The general tried again. He was speaking on behalf of President Johnson, he said. If the people would just write down their grievances, the President would guarantee that the secretaries of the Agriculture and Justice departments would consider them carefully. And if they would give him a list of the homeless people in the room, every effort would be made to find housing.

There was a long silence. Then Mrs. Blackwell spoke. "Mister," she said, "what's wrong with the Delta ain't going to be cured by finding a house for the people in this room. And we been sending pieces of paper up to Washington for three years now, and it ain't done no good. If that's all you got to say, I guess we'll just stay right here."

"But I am authorized to tell you," the general went on, "that Secretary Freeman realizes that Operation HELP

has been delayed, and that the money is being released today to get it going."

He paused. "Now, I have heard your grievances. As an
air force officer I have no power to respond beyond what
I have already communicated. Now I must ask you to leave
quietly."

"We'd like a meeting to discuss it," Isaac Foster told him.

"I'll give you five minutes," the general said.

"We can't have a meeting in five minutes," Isaac said.
"We need half an hour."

"I'll give you twenty minutes," said the general. He
turned on his heel and left, TV cameras, lights, mikes,
cables, and newspaper reporters trailing behind him.

The people locked the door and began talking. But the
meeting came to no conclusion. Some wanted to walk out
immediately; some wanted the air force to perform the
eviction but agreed to offer no resistance. A couple of
white boppers took the hard line, insisting they would resist. They refused the pleas of the others to keep it non-
violent.

Homeless again—the eviction from the air base (*Mary Varela*)

They were still talking twenty minutes later when a billy club shattered the glass of the locked door, spraying broken glass on the people nearby. An airman reached through the broken pane and unlocked the door. Then the air policemen began coming in, four at a time, to carry the demonstrators out.

The people went out the way they said they would: some walked, most were carried, and two or three screamed, fought, and bit.

"Art Thomas," one newspaperman remembers, "went out quietly, riding like a king."

All the troopers were catching verbal abuse—and the Negro troopers had it worst of all. "These are your people, man!" one demonstrator shouted.

A few of the airmen got in some licks, too, using the hidden elbow proddings and pinches a trained policeman learns.

They carried the demonstrators to a patch of frosty grass outside the building, near the gate. A ring of troopers, their clubs gripped in both hands behind them, stood at parade rest to form a human corral surrounding the evicted people.

"We had decided to sit there until the air force forced us to leave," Isaac Foster recalls. "But there were babies with us, and old people, and we were sitting on snow. So we decided to leave.

"And after all, we believed that we had got our message across."

# 8. Beulah Land

---

*"We ain't got nothin' but needs."—Mrs. Ida Mae Lawrence*

---

FOR FIVE MONTHS, the refugees from the air force base sit-in wandered—sometimes literally—in the wilderness.

The day after the eviction they held a news conference in the Greenville DM office. There Mrs. Lawrence and Mrs. Blackwell and Mrs. Foster had wearily told the reporters about their disillusionment with the federal government.

Here are some excerpts from the tape:

Mrs. Blackwell: I feel that the federal government have proven that it don't care about poor people. Everything that we have asked for through these years has been handed down on paper. It's never been a reality. We the poor people of Mississippi is tired. We're tired of it so we're going to build for ourselves, because we don't have a government that represents us.

Mrs. Lawrence: The base is more thought of than the poor peoples was. The buildings weren't doing anything but just sitting there. The building was more respectable than poor hungry peoples with nothing and nowhere to go.

Reporter: Mr. Thomas, why do you think the federal government is afraid to let poor Negroes go ahead and run the [Operation HELP] program?

Rev. Thomas: Nobody is unaware of the power of Congressman Whitten in the House Subcommittee on Agriculture Appropriations. Nobody is unaware of the critical power of John Stennis in the Senate. . . . And those are the kinds of people who are supposed to represent the poor people in Congress.

Mrs. Lawrence: You know, we ain't dumb, even if we are poor. We need jobs. We need food. We need houses. But even with the poverty program we ain't got nothin' but needs.

That's why we was pulled off that building that wasn't being used for anything. We is ignored by the government. The thing about property upset them, but the thing about poor people don't.

So there's no way out but to begin your own beginning, whatever way you can. So far as I'm concerned, that's all I got to say about the past. We're beginning a new future.

They began looking for the new future at Strike City, ten miles east of Greenville. Beech called the man from Atlanta with whom he'd worked in the Selma and Brandon marches, and he bought three huge tents. The group decided to continue calling itself the Poor Peoples' Conference, and to solicit funds for land.

The Strike City people knew what it meant to be homeless, and they had immediately offered space on their five acres to house the air base refugees. But as the week wore on, more and more people arrived from plantations; the word that there was a place for hungry people was still out on the Delta grapevine. And the Freedom Corps, although with considerable misgivings, was following its orders to spread the news on plantations that if you got thrown off or things got too bad, the Delta Ministry had a place for you to go.

In two days, the crowd in the tents had grown to 250 people. There were endless "peoples' meetings," at which Isaac and Mrs. Lawrence and Mrs. Blackwell tried to bring some order and organization to such things as cooking meals and setting up beds.

The Strike City people had managed in the last five months to make themselves reasonably snug in their one-to-a-family squad tents. There was snow still on the ground, but little wood-burning stoves kept the tents warmer than the plantation shacks had been.

Always a close-knit group, they watched the invasion with growing consternation. They saw their new community center, built with the help of University of Pennsylvania students on Christmas vacation just a month before, being used as a mess hall by day and dormitory by night. They saw children just off the plantations drop peanut butter sandwiches and black-eyed peas all over the new floor; restless teenagers roamed the area, peering into the Strike City's peoples' tents, getting into fist fights, and even breaking a couple of the community center windows. The adults in the new group, some of them leaders back home on the plantation, were in no mood to take orders from their new landlords.

Several of the DM people were out looking for land to buy, but weren't having any luck.

Much of the DM staff time, however, was taken up by the federal bureaucrats who had suddenly descended upon the state by the dozens. Stung by the air base publicity, they came demanding time and attention for proposals to solve all the Delta's ills. Briefed and guided around by DM staffers, many of these men eventually got some limited programs into the state for housing, jobs, and training—but when the money did come it was paid through "less controversial" groups than the DM or through local politicians.

As the frustration at Strike City mounted, so did the friction.

On the fifth day, the people in the three big tents got

another eviction notice. This one was from the people of
Strike City.

"We're sorry," one of the strikers said. "But there just
ain't room for all of us on five acres. And all our stuff that
we worked so hard for is being tore up. You got to find
another place."

The "another place" they found will always be known
to those who were there as Mud City.

A Negro farmer in Issaquena County let them set up
the tents on his land while he tried to decide whether to
sell it or not. It was miles off the highway, between plantation hamlets appropriately named Hopedale and Grace,
and the land was so low that a day's rain turned the black
soil into bottomless, gooey sludge. The sun shone the day
they set up the tents. Then it rained every day for two
weeks.

The landowner was being visited by other black farmers
with messages that they had heard the Klan was going to
kill him. Whites in pickup trucks drove by glaring. The
DDT in Greenville helpfully reported the owner's full
name and rural location.

The farm owner finally decided the profits of a good
sale would be no use to him if he were dead. He told the
Poor Peoples' they could stay a little while longer while
they tried to find other land in the county, but that he
would not sell his land. The search continued, as frustrating
as the one in Washington County, as each new interested
landowner was scared off by a visit from white neighbors.

At the same time, the people were getting sick. Half the
adults and most of the children had colds. Virginia Hilton,
an RN, went out to help after hours, and ended up spending two days. The temperatures were sometimes in the high
thirties or low forties all day long, and it was getting harder

to find a dry place at night. Families began drifting away, going off to crowd in with relatives in some town.

The people at Mud City thought about Mount Beulah, where many of them had been in January, just before the air base sit-in. They knew they had an invitation to come there if they wished. So, strong as was the pull toward land of their own, the lure of a dry roof was stronger that cold, rainy week in February.

There had been 250 people at Strike City. About 180 of these stayed long enough to move to Mud City. And late in February, about 125 people packed up the tents and drove in a caravan of Delta Ministry cars seventy-five miles south to Mount Beulah.

Mount Beulah, some of its permanent residents, and the Delta Ministry budget still have not recovered from what is referred to as "the time the Peoples were here." It was a wild, exciting, hopeful, discouraging, dangerous, and thoroughly confusing time.

The families had lived in relative isolation in their scattered plantation shacks. Now twenty families were living together in Medgar's Way, a two-story dormitory. Each family had a room or two of its own, but the noise was deafening.

Most of the adults had spent their lives doing exactly what one or more white folks told them to do during their long working days. Now they were being asked to make their own decisions, to think things out for themselves, and to disagree with anybody on campus, white or black, when they felt like it.

On the plantations they had been in competition with the other families for work—a competition the boss-man encouraged. Now they were being asked to work together as a community, making decisions and imposing disciplines on themselves for the good of the whole. Declaring they would build a new city and their own government was one thing; trying it out was proving to be quite another.

The physical adjustment was almost as difficult as the mental one. Very few plantation shacks had running water. None had indoor toilets, and many didn't have even an outdoor privy. You relieved yourself when and where the necessity came.

Such luxuries as regular bathing or brushing your teeth were out of the question when the nearest clean water was a faucet on a pipe coming up out of the front yard of the neighboring shack, a quarter mile down the road. Some of the families had never used spoons or forks.

Now they found themselves living in buildings with indoor toilets and running water, with sheets on the beds and a bed for each child. They ate in the cafeteria, lining up to get food and sitting down at the table to eat it. They had meat at least once a day, instead of once or twice a month.

The reaction of some visitors and short-time volunteers was predictable: "Why don't you insist that these people clean themselves up and exert some discipline on their children?"

But the truth was that you don't change a lifetime of habits in a few weeks. The staff felt there were more important goals than deodorant sweetness and dainty manners. A far more important step was helping people change the image they had of themselves.

Many of the people of the Poor Peoples' Conference had come subconsciously to believe the white man's assessment of them: they were work animals, slightly less than human, whose only worth was the labor which the bossman, out of his kindness, allowed them to provide. These weren't the tough, independent, skilled tractor drivers of Strike City, who risked losing their jobs in striking for a raise. These were the rejects, the people whose only skill had been grasping a hoe or a cotton boll. Now, because of old age or mechanization or the cotton cutbacks, they were told they were of no use whatsoever to society. Their poor opinion of themselves was only strengthened by the way they had been declared surplus.

Mrs. Eaton and her ten children were told to leave the plantation where she had worked twenty-two years because she was about to have another baby and couldn't work. The baby was three days old when she came to Mount Beulah.

John Hoskins, tall and gaunt at seventy, was forced off a Sunflower County plantation because the owner wouldn't let him work any more, and wouldn't let the children forage for fire wood. It was eighteen degrees the day they left.

Arcola Butler had lived all his life on the same plantation; it had never been necessary for him to learn to read or write.

Mrs. Savannah Williams had been a life long resident of a Bolivar County plantation, where neither she nor any of her children had ever attended school. It was a one-room shack, too far away from school to walk, and there was no bus. Besides, the owner had never encouraged people to attend. She left because there was no more work for her.

A few of the PPC members had left their homes voluntarily. Casey Robinson was a tractor driver who joined the group at Mud City. Mrs. Ora D. Wilson had been a day laborer for twenty-two years; the mother of eight children, she had been cut off welfare in Indianola after demonstrating at the state capitol in 1965. Mrs. Lawrence was a midwife and a long-time activist from Rosedale; she had helped plan and lead the air base sit-in.

Many of the mothers kept their rooms spotless; keeping

all eight or ten noses wiped was more difficult. The women did come to scrub the dining hall floor each day, and set up a reasonably effective counterattack on flies. But except for the requirements of health (there were classes, with refresher sessions, on how to flush the toilet and brush the teeth), it was agreed that the changes taking place in the daily "citizenship classes" were far more important.

These twice-daily sessions in Till Hall were a combination of town meeting, gripe fest, confessional, and lecture course. Discussion might range from the current efforts to buy land to the question of whether PPC members should have guns in their rooms. DM staff members might be asked to give instruction in simple arithmetic, or might be told to stay out of a session altogether.

It was hard for many PPC members to take part. Most had never spoken up in a group, except to recite a testimony at church. Now they were being asked to speak their minds, often in the presence of white people.

Leon Howell, an NCC staff member from New York, received permission to attend one of the sessions. His report in *Christianity and Crisis* includes this evidence of the wide gap the classes tried to bridge:

"As I, the only white in the room, took my seat, a middle-aged Negro, eyes downcast, apology all over his face—a shuffling caricature of a man—said to me, a total stranger, 'Would ya ' scuse me, mistah? Ah'm jist gonna git sumpin to smoke. Be right back to class, Ah shore will.'

"Within the hour, an older, illiterate woman stopped the class proceedings, looked straight across the room at me, and demanded; 'Can somebody tell me what this strange white man doin' h'yah?' "

No matter what the topic under discussion, the really important work of the classes at Beulah was the progress people made from the latter response to the former—from lifelong subservience to open, even belligerent, independence.

It took the group two weeks to decide what to grow on the land to which they'd be moving. Word had finally come that a planter near Greenville would sell his four hundred acres, and that a wealthy friend of DM in New York would lend the PPC $71,000 for the down payment.

The first decision about a crop took only minutes: there would be no cotton grown! The people had picked all the cotton they ever wanted to see. Alternate suggestions ranged from tomatoes to soybeans.

After several days of arguing, the group decided to ask Clarence Hall, the DM staff member who was an Issaquena County farmer, for his advice.

Mr. Hall checked the county agent's map, ran soil tests, and reported that soybeans was the logical choice. After another four or five days of discussion, the people agreed.

While the PPC agonized over what to plant, how to answer the telephone, how to make change, and how to collect the laundry, the DM staff was doing some soul-searching too.

The dream of a free city had been kicking around for a long time. On Warren McKenna's office wall, almost from the day he moved in, was a full-color aerial view of an Israeli *moshav*—a cooperative village where the people owned their own land but farmed it cooperatively. Miss Marian Wright, the attractive young legal Defense Fund attorney who sat on the DM Commission, had spent time in Israel studying the *moshav*. And as the floundering movement looked for new goals, the trend toward independence from the white liberal, toward economic development, toward something more meaningful than the *Better Homes and Gardens* way of life—all these seemed to fit in with the "new city" idea.

The trouble was, the idea became a reality before anybody was ready for it. There had been some long bull sessions on the subject, but the DM staff, at least, was simply not prepared to have 150 people and four hundred acres of land on its hands. In the turbulent days during and right after the air base sit-in, discussion was hot and long.

Many of the staff flatly opposed the idea. Even if it would work, they said, Delta Ministry—living as it did from month to month with no assurance of continued existence—would be irresponsible to make any promises for the future to plantation people. The Freedom Corps kids, who had never turned down a job because it was too dangerous, refused to do any more recruiting for what was then being called "New City." SNCC, CORE, and COFO were gone; the flurry of federal interest after the air base sit-in was waning; the Freedom Corps knew that the history of Mississippi was one of broken promises from helpful outsiders. They weren't going to be part of what inevitably would be another fiasco.

Their doubts about DM's longevity were reinforced by the activities of the NCC's evaluation committee, which had held its first meeting just ten days before the air base incident. In the spring, egged on by everybody in the country who ever had complaints about DM, the committee was taking testimony from such widely varied witnesses as Governor Johnson, Aaron Henry, the people of Strike City, and the editor of the Jackson *Clarion-Ledger*.

The very fact that DM was under investigation was enough to make several denominations hesitant; they were withholding a commitment of 1966 funds until the report was in. And meantime, the cost just of feeding the PPC was threatening to run through the available money by August.

But those who argued *for* the idea also had both practical and philosophical reasons. The practical one was very real: the people were at Mount Beulah and they had no place else to go. You couldn't just evict 150 people, the way the plantation owners had.

The philosophical one, hammered out in long, noisy staff sessions, reflected many of the ideas which in a few months would be put into slogan form as "black power."

The "new community," the staff felt, "is a viable alternative to present conditions all over the state. . . . The Negro will look to the acquisition of political power as a legitimate and necessary goal, but now reinforced with an independent economic base."

It should be clear that the new community approach is not an attempt at protective isolation (new ghettoes), or to provide an alternative to political realities (utopias). It is a base for the practice of democracy and the development of full citizenship sufficient to contribute to a new Mississippi.

We are not proposing some perfect city but a community of men, women and children engaged in the process of becoming free —socially, educationally, economically, politically, spiritually.

The staff went on to make these comments about the state of the Freedom Movement in Mississippi:

1. The freedom movement has been largely an integration movement: the attempt of the Negro to attain "equal" participation and recognition at all levels of American society.

2. There is little evidence (north or south) that American society is yet prepared to accept anything more than tokenism or to accept creatively the possible contributions of the Negro community.

3. The strategies and achievements of the movement itself have raised the real question of whether freedom can be equated with the contemporary middle class standard of life: the question of whether acceptance into the system is desirable.

4. The so-called "second phase" of the movement, often es-

poused, emphasizes the need for the Negro to develop educational, economic and political skills and power. . . . But current self-help programs such as cooperatives, home industry, adult literacy, while providing a small measure of economic experience and hope, do little to counter the vastness of the whole problem of poverty.

5. Almost all government programs for "uplift" fail to reach the poor Negro and if they do, do so on a paternalistic basis. The poor remain poor and dependent.

6. The poor black's participation in the "second phase" is still severely hampered because of the continuing dependence upon the white power structure for basic economic aid. The pattern has been for the system to cut its aid to the Negro community when it becomes a threat. . . . Until there is a break in the economic ties that bind the movement to the system, there can be no real breakthrough at other social, political and cultural levels.

The staff emphasized that it was self-determination, not self-sufficiency, that they hoped for the new community. For a long time, outside funds would be needed, but the people of the community itself must determine how the money would be used.

One source of this outside money was supposed to be the federal government. The Office of Economic Opportunity, in the furor right after the air base incident, had asked DM to submit a proposal for a self-help housing and education program. The project, written to fit OEO's suggestions, was to provide a year's intensive training for fifty to one hundred families, plus the materials and training to build their own homes.

The question of whether or not to apply for federal money was the subject of another hot staff discussion—can you beat the system with the system's own money?—but the decision was to apply. Then, month after month, as DM's financial fortunes looked more and more grim, the OEO program became more and more important to the future of Freedom City. And month after month the word out of Washington was that Stennis, Whitten, *et al.*, were still blocking the grant.

Late in March, amidst all this confusion and uncertainty, a brand-new problem nearly blew the whole program sky high.

Armed with pistols, a group of the boppers—wandering, rootless, young civil rights workers who follow the action—invaded the campus to "free" the PPC people from Delta Ministry influence.

Before the thing was over, several DM staffers had been shot at, several families left the PPC in fear for their lives, and eight black Mississippians had picketed the Church Center at the United Nations in New York in the mistaken belief that the NCC headquarters was there.

The boppers had first come to the air force base in January. Insecure, belligerent, and feeling very much the confusion prevalent in the movement over goals, most of them had been trouble from the start. (In discussions inside the building at the air base, one white bopper had challenged the right of Isaac Foster, Mrs. Lawrence, and Mrs. Blackwell—all poor, black, native Mississippians—to be spokesmen. "The local people have to speak," he insisted again and again.) It was the boppers who had refused to be nonviolent as the air policemen carried them out.

At Mud City, a bopper with a foghorn voice had nearly ruined the chance for nationwide publicity—and resulting financial support for the PPC—by demanding that a CBS camera crew pay each man, woman, and child who appeared in the picture. The argument lasted more than an hour before some PPC members lifted him bodily and carried him away.

At Beulah, the handful of boppers who had not drifted away were just hanging around, eating the free meals and criticizing the PPC and DM. Nobody paid much attention until Art Thomas, under continual pressure to save money, told them they would be expected to help with the PPC program if they wanted to continue enjoying free room and board at Beulah.

At this "fascistic" act, as one young man described it, the boppers set to work undermining the peoples' faith in Art and the DM staff. Each night they caucused with PPC members, criticizing the day's program and spreading doubts about DM's intentions. One night they kicked down doors in the dormitories and waved their pistols at the surprised inhabitants, some of whom had refused to swallow the boppers' stories.

One night, after Charles Horwitz had had words with one of the boppers, a bullet came whistling through his bedroom window. It missed him by inches.

A meeting of the poor people, with the announced purpose of discussing the use of guns on campus, was broken up by one of the boppers—waving a pistol.

For a week the campus was in terror. Many of the plantation people refused to come to meetings for fear of getting shot.

It was not a situation where you could call in the sheriff. That worthy had already told Art never to call him if there was trouble: "Call the FBI. They're your special buddies." The advice of the FBI on one previous occasion when they'd been notified was, "Call the sheriff. This is not a federal matter." Besides, the people making this trouble were still movement people. They were still mostly Mississippi Negroes. In addition to the obvious dangers to them, filing charges against the boppers would have permanently damaged DM's relationships within the movement. "We have to deal with them as people whose concerns are as real as our own," Art told me one night, a few hours after one of them had taken a shot at him. Besides, Art had known some of the boppers since the hellish summers of 1963 and 1964; the emotional problems behind their actions now were undoubtedly related to the dangers they had faced then.

During all this, one group of younger PPC members had been in New York City raising money. They included the three daughters of Johnnie Boyd, who sang gospel and freedom songs wherever somebody could round up an audience for them. The group's return to Mount Beulah had been postponed several times, although the size of the checks they were sending back indicated that the lure of big city life had more to do with the postponement than any hope of making PPC financially stable.

The boppers got word to the Indianola Sunshine Singers and friends that DM was mistreating the Poor Peoples. They also suggested looking up some friends in the Progressive Labor Party, a group whose philosophy puts it well to the left of everybody but Chairman Mao himself.

The PLP welcomed the Mississippians, provided lodging so they could extend their stay, and helped them print leaflets:

## NATIONAL COUNCIL OF CHURCHES
## EXPLOITS
## MISERY OF MISSISSIPPI BLACK PEOPLE

This is the office of the National Council of Churches, which has a local branch in Mississippi known as the " Delta Ministry."

You have heard of the Poor People's Conference and many saw this group on nationwide television Feb. 2nd. when they did a live-in at the Greenville Air Force Base. They are a group of Afro-Americans who have been thrown off the plantations and are homeless, not to mention jobless.

The Delta Ministry is pretending to come to the aid of these people, but its real purpose is to control their life. It gave them land to live on; this land belonged to an old College called Mt. Bulath located in Edwards, Mississippi. The all white staff lives in the campus white mansion while the people live in the dormitories.

When word got around the country that these people needed funds for food and clothing large sums of money throughout the nation were raised and sent to the Delta Ministry Staff, and the Poor People's Conference never saw one dime of it. When the people started to challenge the leadership, and ask the Delta Ministry Staff to work in the background and let the people determine their own policies and handle their own program, the Delta Ministry gave the Poor People's Conference a bill of $20,000 presumably for food and tents because that is all they received from them and proceeded to evict the people from Mt. Bulath.

These 8 representatives of the Poor People's Conference are inside sitting in to tell them they won't allow this unjust act to continue and we picket outside to support their just struggle.

SUPPORT STRUGGLE OF AFRO-AMERICAN
PEOPLE OF MISSISSIPPI

SPONSORED BY: THE POOR PEOPLE'S CONFERENCE OF MISSISSIPPI
FOR FURTHER INFORMATION CONTACT

WEST SIDE UNIFIED ACTION COUNCIL
100 West 82nd Street, New York

The first use of the leaflets was a dud; the group handed them out at the Church Center for the UN—approximately ninety blocks from the NCC headquarters near Grant's Tomb on Riverside Drive.

Art Thomas and Jon Regier met with the group the next day and tried to get them to return to Beulah to see for themselves that the charges weren't true. There were more Negroes than whites on the DM staff, and more black people than white living in the old mansion that was Mount Beulah's headquarters. The money solicited by DM came to a special post office box, which was opened daily by Mrs. Lawrence of the PPC; she kept the records and deposited the money. There was no bill for $20,000; the PPC had, in an open meeting back at Strike City, agreed to try to repay a loan of $4000 for the tents if resources ever permitted. There *was* an eviction; the Freedom Corps men had ejected, with explicit threats and the waving of a lead pipe or two, a couple of the boppers who had been most troublesome.

The group of young PPC members hesitantly agreed to go back to Mississippi to find out for themselves what was happening. But a few days later, in an open-air rally at Columbia University, a speaker for the group announced a "live-in" at the Interchurch Center for March 10, and invited students to take part.

The staid, gray Interchurch Center was all nerves that day. Employees had been notified about the possibility of a demonstration. Key staff members were stationed at the elevator on each floor, with strict orders to treat the demonstrators courteously and to try to persuade them to come to the fifth-floor conference room.

The pickets didn't arrive until 4 P.M. By that time Mrs. Blackwell, Mrs. Lawrence, and Johnnie Boyd of the PPC had arrived from Mississippi, along with Curtis Hayes of the DM staff. Mr. Boyd was not only emerging as one of the leaders of the PPC, but was the father of three teen-age girls who were part of the picket line.

The pickets were greeted at the front entrance to the Interchurch Center by Mr. Boyd, the stern parent, and Mr. Hayes, the former SNCC field worker and Freedom Corps director. They agreed to talk. The discussions went on for five hours, in true movement fashion.

First they refuted the charges on the leaflet. Then they got down to the real discussion: how serious was the National Council of Churches about its long-term commitment to Mississippi? By the time it was over, the pickets were ready to go home, where the remaining issues could be argued out in the daily town meetings on the Beulah campus.

It was a wild spring, and it seemed like an endless one. The final figures were in on the 1965 DM budget, and it looked as though DM had overspent by more than 50 percent. With expectation of even less income in 1966, there were some drastic cuts. DM had been supporting the Freedom Information Service, a six-member staff which tried to coordinate and make available information to all parts of the movement in Mississippi. In May, our support had to stop. The McComb office, opened amidst the bombings a year and a half before, was closed without a bang. The Freedom Corps was pared to three young men, all of whom were involved in the PPC program.

As soon as the four hundred acres—"the land," the people called it—was available, the men at Beulah began making daily round trips of 150 miles to get the soybeans planted and prepare the housing. They built wooden platforms, on which prefabricated, tent-like plastic shelters were erected.

The new shelters didn't look very strong, but they were guaranteed to last four to seven years, and they cost only $500 apiece. By writing letters to everybody he knew in the North, Warren McKenna had managed to come up with the cash to buy twenty-four of them.

The people finally came to the land in July. Of the caravan from Beulah that day, at least three cars were stopped and given summonses by the state cop who habitually followed our people.

The women hadn't seen the new houses yet. Some of them shook their heads and, like the children of Israel at the Canaan border, announced that they'd rather go back to Beulah. But there were others who had tears in their eyes as they stood looking at the circle of snow-white huts, like wagons drawn up for protection against the Indians. "Well," Mrs. Lawrence said, "we're finally here."

# 9. Freedom City

*"I have had my bitters and sweets here."*—Mrs. Ora D.
*Wilson*, FREEDOM CITY

THE FIRST SUMMER at Freedom City was a hot one
and full of frustrations. One source of trouble was the shiny
new houses themselves. Made of urethane plastic over a
corrugated cardboard base about an inch thick, the houses
arrived all folded up like accordions. The two halves were
unfolded and fastened to the base of raw lumber the men
had already built; then prefabricated end pieces containing
a door and windows were clipped in place. The finished
product looked like a tent created out of paper by an
origami hobbyist. It was supposed to last five years.

But as they set up housekeeping, the wives found that
not all the parts fit correctly; if water wasn't coming in
through the cracks, then dust was. With its usual foresight
and efficiency, DM had selected a site which turned out—
after the first rain—to be the lowest and muddiest spot on
the whole farm. The women fought a losing battle against
the mud, which clung in huge gobs to everybody's shoes.

They couldn't get electricity either. The men who were supposed to hook up the newly installed electric system— one naked light bulb per house—stalled and broke appointments and raveled red tape. At the same time, we were having no luck in getting insurance on the houses and the farm buildings. This was understandable but worrisome, since unfriendly whites kept up a steady traffic past the place, and the farmhouse and tractor barn were quite close to the road.

The soybean crop, subject of so much discussion back at Beulah, was a source of frustration, too. By the time the people got settled, it was very late for planting. The weather was bad; it didn't rain enough, and when it did, it was at the wrong time.

But the main hindrance to a good crop wasn't the weather. It was the people. After a lifetime of being told exactly what to do and where, the PPC men found themselves having to exert initiative. They had to decide whether or not to get up in the morning and whether or not to go to work if they did get up. They had to decide who would drive the three tractors and who would use hoes. Somebody had to cook, and somebody else had to babysit while most of the adults were out weeding the long rows of beans.

The sun poured down waves of heat, which went shimmering back up from the dry ground and the dusty beans. Many of the people stayed in the relative cool of their houses. Isaac Foster and Casey Robinson and one or two others got up at dawn and headed for the fields, but their example didn't do much to encourage a whole crew.

Isaac was on the Delta Ministry payroll as Freedom City project director, and he steadfastly refused to order the people to work, or to make their decisions for them. The rest of the DM staff agreed with him. You don't learn self-reliance and self-government by having decisions made for you, they reasoned; learning to be really free also involved the danger of making mistakes.

By the end of the summer, a majority of the people were participating in the PPC meetings, helping organize the work, and were doing their share in the fields. But the fields were choked with weeds, and there was too much catching up to do. The crop was a failure, bringing in barely enough money to pay for seed and fertilizer.

The long-term answer to Freedom City's needs wasn't farming anyway. The idea had always been to bring in industry—small home industry first, and then a larger plant willing to train workers. The presence of a growing factory would in turn make it possible to invite more plantation refugees to come to Freedom City to live and work.

But we had no more success with this hope than we did with the beans. One hot afternoon in Washington, officials of the Economic Development Administration and the Small Business Administration told us we were competing with 14,000 other towns and cities for every factory seeking a location. Besides, we could give no assurance to the management of any company that the state government or the Mississippi Economic Council would welcome a company affiliated in any way with the Delta Ministry. Al Winham, the New England pastor who had been in Mississippi almost continuously since 1964, was DM's director of economic development—a job which involved him in numerous long and usually fruitless trips to Washington and meetings with industrialists.

One major food processing company seemed interested in establishing a canning or freezing plant at Freedom City; it would provide a market and an incentive for Negro landowners to switch from cotton to more profitable produce, fruits and vegetables. But first, the company representative explained, a feasibility study would be conducted—and that would take four years.

Al persuaded the operators of a company which breeds white mice by the tens of thousands for laboratory use to visit Freedom City; they were interested in establishing a branch. Another visitor was looking for people who could make cane-bottom chairs for sale in Kentucky as authentic mountain handicraft. Al made trips to the Midwest to talk to a company president who trains unskilled workers to fabricate simple sheet metal parts in small plants he establishes anywhere in the country.

All these people were interested. But in the end, none of them brought employment to Freedom City. Whether it was the primitive conditions, the extent of the training needed, or the fear of an environment hostile to their business, each one decided to try elsewhere.

Al was having about the same success with the self-help housing proposal OEO had suggested right after the air base incident. Senator Stennis' opposition to the grant, we were told by "informed sources" in Washington, was loud and clear. And President Johnson, who faced growing opposition to United States involvement in Vietnam, was less and less likely to antagonize the senator whose Subcommittee on Preparedness could give him—or refuse him—more soldiers in Vietnam.

So the people of Freedom City waited to see what would happen to this latest promise of the white men in Washington, only half believing that this time would be the exception—that the promise would be kept.

September arrived, and time for school. The people got a chuckle out of what happened. Negroes around Glen Allan, twenty miles southwest of Freedom City, had signed up scores of parents under "freedom of choice" to send their children to the all-white grade school there. The black kids outnumbered the white kids on registration day. The next day, although the date for choosing a school had passed, the school board allowed all the white parents to transfer their children to the white Avon school, sixteen miles away.

The first chuckle belonged to the Negro parents around Glen Allan; for years their children had been getting up at 6 A.M. and waiting in the cold for a bus to take them to a school an hour and a half away. Now it was the white kids' turn, while many of the black kids could walk to school! The second chuckle belonged to the Freedom City parents, who delivered thirty-seven children to the Avon School for registration the day the white children from Glen Allan came to escape integration.

The decision to put the Freedom City children in a white school was a tough one, and one which continued to be debated all winter. Many of the children had never been in school at all; there were two thirteen-year-olds in the first grade. Even the ones who had been in school were three to five years behind their new classmates, because the Jim Crow schools were that bad.

The teachers were patient and seemed to be trying to be fair to the Freedom City children. This wasn't always easy, since a punch in the nose was the common means for settling juvenile arguments at Freedom City. The style of young life on the plantations had been a lot rougher, noisier, and less formal than that of the white bosses' children with whom they now shared a classroom. Besides, the independent spirit which was the aim of the whole Freedom City project had blossomed with a vengeance in the children; they were not about to accept any slighting remark, real or imagined, from a white person—classmate or teacher. So, with a frequency far more than their numbers war-

ranted, the Freedom City kids were making command appearances in the principal's office. The white children were
not as fair as the teachers, and there was a lot of petty
harassment.

Any hopes of solving the problem of catching up with
the white children centered in the Freedom City cafeteria.
From 5 to 7:30 each night, Rims Barber, Sue Geiger, Pat
Mutch, and others sat down with the schoolchildren in the
cafeteria and helped them do their homework. It took
patience they didn't know they had to work with second-
graders who couldn't count and fifth-graders who couldn't
read. At first the staff hoped to include Negro history and
some art projects that might encourage imagination. But
it soon became obvious that it would take all the energy of
all the volunteers available just to help the children keep up
with their assigned grades.

The tutoring sessions were to go on all winter, moving
from the cafeteria to one of the abandoned farm shacks,
and then to a specially partitioned classroom in the barn.
Eventually two Negro teachers from Greenville joined the
tutoring staff—an essential addition in a project which
wanted the children to learn that black can be just as smart
as white. By the time the school year was over, one nine-
year-old boy who had never been in school before had pro-
gressed through the first three grades. And half of the
original thirty-seven chlidren, despite suspensions, harassment, and discouragement, finished the school year with
passing grades.

The damp, chilly fall did little to raise spirits at Freedom
City. Isaac Foster, who had already delayed starting college
for two years because of the plantation strike and then
Freedom City, finally left for Queens College in New
York. He left a big hole in the staff.

Born on the plantation and educated in a tin shack until

he was thirteen, Isaac had come through the murder of his father and the pressures of the system with amazingly little bitterness. He had been graduated from high school at the top of his class despite a schedule which was interrupted for chopping and picking seasons. He had somehow shucked off the heavy Delta accent without losing the power to move men with words or to get in and work beside them. He had been the chairman of Mississippi Freedom Labor Union Local Four when it struck the Andrews plantation and co-chairman of the Poor Peoples' Conference when they invaded the air base.

One night just before he left the land, he stood watching the school children sitting with their tutors in the cafeteria. "Up until about '61 or '62," he told me, "we went to school in the church house. And there was one teacher who taught everybody from the first through the twelfth grade. And the teacher herself had finished, say, maybe the sixth, seventh, eighth grade in that same church house herself. That's all.

"These kids here are going to know how to say 'He does.' My teacher said the book was wrong, and made me say, 'He do.'"

Isaac's job on the DM staff as Freedom City project director was taken by John Bradford, a Roman Catholic layman who had been a SNCC organizer in Hattiesburg and in the little all-Negro hamlet of Winstonville. He had attended Ohio State University for a while and had worked for the CDGM Head Start program.

Bradford wasn't the leader that Isaac was, but he stayed with the job through days that would have unbalanced somebody less tough. And the people themselves were assuming more of the leadership.

The rains and gloomy skies which came that fall—too

late to do the beans any good—were hard enough on morale. But it soon got worse. Two more irreplaceable men, who had molded the life of the Delta Ministry and of the Poor Peoples' Conference, left the staff and left Mississippi. They were Art Thomas and Warren McKenna.

Art had been in Europe most of July and August, enjoying his first vacation in three years and attending the Church and Society Conference in Geneva. When he came back, he stayed only long enough to resign.

Warren had long before promised his family back in Boston that he would stay with DM only two years—until December 1966. We never found out whether he actually would have resigned then; in early September a letter came from New York informing him he would be, in the gobbledy-gook of church bureaucratic language, "terminated" in fifteen days.

It was too much all at once. Art had directed DM since its first day; more than any other single person he had determined the tone and direction it would take. He had fought the staff, the DM commission, and the New York supervisors in order to make Freedom City the major item of the DM program in 1966.

Warren was the dreamer and planner. He had put together the rationale for Freedom City, and was the man on the staff who took time to look far down the road to see where the movement was going.

The reaction of the Freedom City people was one of bewilderment. "We thought the Delta Ministry was going to stay," Mrs. Lawrence said. "They had that meeting in New York. Now everybody's leaving. What's happening?"

The reaction of the DM staff was anger, growing out of the suspicion that both Art and Warren had been victims of denominational pressure. The NCC program board had assured its constituents, after the June evaluation committee report, that there would be a tightening of administrative procedures. DM's critics, especially the Methodist bishop and conference superintendents in Mississippi, had interpreted this to mean that some of the staff members most repugnant to them would be fired. The fact that most of us would never know for sure did not help ease the anger any. Neither did a flying visit from three of the New York executives who assured us that Art had left of his own free will, and that Warren's early termination resulted from money troubles, not denominational politics.

The staff was still stewing over this frustrating confrontation (Warren stayed fired), worrying over the increasing complaints and tension at Freedom City, and trying to ensure a decent vote for the Reverend Clifton Whitley, a Negro Methodist minister who was running for James Eastland's senate seat, when another blow came. Mrs. Lawrence, president of the PPC, and my wife, Ginny, who was the Freedom City nurse, were seriously injured in an auto accident.

They had taken Mrs. Berdie Hoskins to Vicksburg, eighty-five miles away, to give birth to her baby in the

Mrs. Wilson's house, and everything she owns, the morning after the storm at Freedom City (*Ken Thompson*)

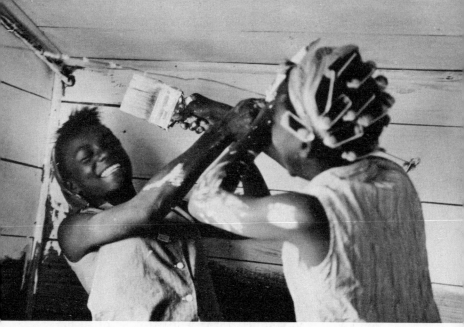

Painting the cafeteria at Freedom City (*Nash Basom*)

charity hospital there. The hospital in Greenville was refusing charity patients because its federal funds had been cut off for non-compliance with the desegregation laws.

On the way back, after a night spent without sleep because the receptionist wouldn't let them sit—one white, one black—in the waiting room, Ginny and Mrs. Lawrence were run off the road by a woman who drove out of a side road without looking. Our car, with Ginny driving, flipped end over end down the embankment and was demolished. Ginny had a concussion and torn back muscles which still plague her; Mrs. Lawrence had head cuts which required forty-two stitches.

The young lady who caused the accident, though her car wasn't hit, became hysterical. She was comforted by the investigating state trooper, who was a family friend, by her father, who was the deputy sheriff, and by her uncle, who was the state legislator from that county.

On their second day in the hospital Ginny received a citation for reckless driving from the trooper, and on the eighth day, before either woman had even been out of bed, their doctor discharged them from the hospital after making some obscure and rather apologetic comments about the strange ways of Mississippi politics. (There was no thought of fighting the reckless driving charge. The judge in whose court the case would be heard owned a store in which one of our volunteers had been beaten—with two ribs broken—a month before.)

Freedom City didn't need any more trouble. But on November 10, while their president and their nurse were still in the hospital and Senator Eastland was celebrating his re-election (under the slogan, "If you are not at the polls, you know who will be!"), the worst trouble of all hit.

The houses blew down.

A line squall came across the Delta around 1 A.M., with seventy-five-mile-an-hour winds and driving sheets of rain. It lifted two of the houses right off their platforms and whirled them away like kites. It buckled and tore the others until rain poured in through large holes. It made uninhabitable the only home Mrs. Wilson had ever owned, the house Clay Miller's wife had kept spotless despite the mud, the homes of the Williamses, the Eatons, the Lawrences, the Robinsons.

When the front had passed (it would still be strong enough to knock down trees that noon when it hit Atlanta), the people of Freedom City were surrounded by their rain-soaked belongings, ruined furniture, and useless houses.

Following everything else the way it did, the storm could have been the end of Freedom City. Instead, it was the point at which the project hit bottom and started back up.

The disaster got the people cooperating; there was a community spirit of a kind the group hadn't achieved before. In the cold November dawn, clear after the rain, families helped one another, carrying the salvaged remnants of belongings to shelter. They crowded into the cafeteria and into the two frame buildings that were livable.

We kept the phones in the Greenville office busy that day, asking for help. Through Francis Stevens, a white Jackson attorney, we contacted Civil Defense and the Red Cross. Two CD men were on the scene before noon and, after surveying the damage, promised to send bedding for that night and lumber to build temporary shelter.

That was before they talked to the state welfare department, however. We were informed later in the day that after these discussions the Civil Defense men had decided they were unable to help.

I called the Reverend Bob Fulton, pastor of one of the most liberal congregations in town—First Presbyterian. He was one of the few white clergymen ever to visit our office, and had seemed genuinely, if cautiously, interested. And today he seemed truly sorry as he said, "Bruce, I wish there were something we could do. But I don't dare ask my congregation to help the Delta Ministry—not even with blankets and food for a need like this. There's still too much resentment toward you folks."

The local Red Cross executive had failed to return our calls. But a friend of DM's, the president of a Red Cross chapter in Vermont, got through to her by long distance. He was told that the Greenville Red Cross would offer no help, for four reasons (all untrue): the Freedom City people had been involved in the Lafayette Park tent-in in Washington, D.C., eight months before; the Red Cross had not been advised of any need; this was just a stunt to get free blankets; the people at Freedom City were "wards" of the National Council of Churches.

We never did get any Red Cross help, but the incident led to a couple of interesting examples of bureaucratic double-talk from regional and national offices of that organization—a demonstration of the fear which anything controversial instills in the hearts of those who depend upon the public, business, or industry for financial support.

An Indiana pastor had written a friend who was an assistant regional manager of the Red Cross, asking why there had been no help for Freedom City. In reply, the friend quoted a "survey" by the Washington County chapter, which reported that only two or three houses had been destroyed and only four more had received "minor damage." More important, according to the letter, was the report that the people stored their food and clothing in a common building, and thus there was "no *individual* need requiring Red Cross assistance."

The Reverend Garnett Day, a Disciples of Christ national staff member who has organized several food drives for the Delta, saw the letter. He wrote to the National Red Cross:

"I was present on the spot several hours after the storm and witnessed the disaster. Fifteen homes were either totally demolished or damaged beyond use. This would indicate, it seems, that your Washington County Chapter cannot be relied on to investigate disaster situations."

The reply from national headquarters contained a new explanation—and a phrase which ought to win some kind of prize for bureaucratic rationalization. The unfortunate situation in Freedom City was not caused by a "disaster"; it occurred because the plastic houses at Freedom City were totally unsuitable for winter weather. Thus their collapse could not be considered a disaster. This unsuitability had been verified, the letter solemnly added, by the weather bureau and by "responsible people." Therefore, it said, the

Red Cross did not assume responsibility for helping those who were homeless.

There were concerned people who did help. I called Mrs. Porter Brown, executive secretary of the Board of Missions of the Methodist Church, at the denomination's General Conference in Chicago. Within hours she was reporting a $6000 donation made jointly by the Methodists and the Evangelical United Brethren at that conference. Garnett Day, who had been on the scene, got trucks of food and clothing rolling from a collection depot in Maryland.

With some of the money we were able to insulate the barn, wire it for electricity, and divide it into four large apartments. Two families moved into each of the share-croppers' shacks, which had been empty since the PPC bought the land. The shacks were first made snug against the weather, but there was something distasteful about the idea. The people had come a long way, and this seemed too much like going back.

Yes, they spent Christmas in the barn. Forty-seven of them, including thirty-five children. The parallel with the original Christmas was too obvious to miss. People from all over the country sent money, toys, and clothing. Even white merchants in Greenville joined in, making donations of toys and clothing along with fervent pleas for anonymity.

The new year continued to bring new hope. Mrs. Barnes found that the old frame Elks Club could be bought, cut into three pieces, and moved the ten miles to the land for $4000. Somewhere she wangled the money, and each of the three buildings made two large, comfortable apartments. We needed another $2000 to finish and furnish the three buildings. A radio appeal for the purpose was made in Holland and listeners there donated $11,000. The people moved out of the barn.

The word out of Washington continued to be that Sargent Shriver was ready to make the self-help housing grant. It awaited only the announcement by the big philanthropic foundation which would contribute the $150,000 for building materials, so the announcements could be made together.

But the foundation was interested in legislation then before the Senate, and was afraid that a grant to a group associated with the Delta Ministry might cost the support of southern senators. The announcement was delayed through January, then week by week through February. Finally, on March 30—thirteen months after the OEO itself had suggested the program—the telegram came to Clarence Hall, chairman of Delta Opportunities Corporation.

The OEO money, Clarence explained to the people on the land, totalled $199,805. It would be spent on recruiting and training fifty families off plantations. The training would include basic adult education—literacy, arithmetic, reading blueprints, and so on. It would also include such trades as carpentry, masonry, wiring, and plumbing.

With their training, and the $176,000 in materials donated by the foundation the families would build their own homes on eighty of the four hundred acres of Freedom City. During the training, the families would receive a weekly salary and live at Freedom City. Delta Opportunities Corporation, governed by a board of black Mississippians from nine Delta counties, had been organized with DM's help to administer such grants.

The people had already begun making plans for the small shops and services needed by a community of three hundred to four hundred people, and those Freedom City pioneers who didn't qualify for the OEO training would be involved in those projects.

By summer, when the DOC board began hiring people to staff the housing project, Freedom City had become a different place. The long, drawn-out wait, always with the subconscious knowledge that white men don't keep their promises, was over—and this time the promise had been kept. The people pitched in, without promise of pay or success, and cleared a part of their woods as a park for the use of workers on the surrounding plantations. They launched an energetic voter-registration campaign, covering miles around. Much of the complaining and backbiting, the inter-family fighting, ended.

As the year 1967 moved on, almost incredibly uneventful as compared to 1966, Freedom City changed even visually. It became integrated.

A white family, poor plantation workers, came to the PPC and asked to be admitted. There was a hot discussion. Some members, exploited all their lives by whites, were against the idea. "They better be ready to fight if they move in next to me," one lady said. But in the end, the PPC voted yes. "We accept anybody, long as they's poor and willing to work."

The family came and stayed. Two months later, a second white family came. At this writing, both are still a part of Freedom City, pulling their load, getting the same treatment as anybody else.

Why did they come? Jim Alan tried to write it down for *The PPC Speaks*, the mimeographed paper irregularly issued on the land:

We came to Freedom City because we needed help, we was in a bad condition and did not have anywhere else to go.

I have lived on the farm most of my life working for nothing. The rich man has always treated me like dirt because I am poor.

My family and I really like Freedom City. My children are enjoying themselves; we are being treated with dignity and respect. My family and I are looking forward to a better life in the future than the one we have had in the past.

And where did they come from? That's the supreme irony, as Freedom City looks forward to a long and integrated life. The two white families who came seeking help were off the Andrews plantation; they were among the out-of-state workers imported two years before to replace John Henry Sylvester and the MFLU strikers.

# 10. Those Delta Ministers

*"The Delta Ministry is a disgrace to the state of Missis-*
*sippi. Personally I wish all of you would leave the state.*
*"This so-called ministry shows no respect to my Bishop*
*who has charge of this territory.*
*"Do you call that Christian?*
*"I am against anything the NCC stands for."—Letter from*
*a minister,* CARTHAGE, MISSISSIPPPI

B EN  B R O W N  was born black in Mississippi, but he
never could accept the "place" Mississippi wanted to give
him as an inferior citizen.

As a boy in grade school, he told his parents he didn't
like to hear them always saying "yessuh" and "yes ma'am"
to the white folks. In high school, he helped organize a
boycott of the downtown stores in Jackson because of the
way they treated Negro customers.

He was sixteen when the early freedom riders came
through Mississippi, desegregating bus stations. When they
were brutally beaten, Ben was among the handful of students who demonstrated in protest.

Two years later Medgar Evers was shot down in the
driveway of his home in Jackson; Ben again was among the
few who dared to make a public protest.

During the long, hot summer of 1964, fresh out of high school, Ben worked for COFO in voter registration. He kept an irregular twenty-hour day, eating poorly and at odd hours, but the association gave him a new understanding of what was happening in Mississippi.

The Jackson police got to know him as a civil rights agitator, and harassed him regularly. His mother, frightened for his life, tried to get him to go live with an aunt in Chicago. He refused.

In the next four years he was arrested seven times for civil rights activities.

In 1965, he was among the one thousand people arrested for picketing the all-white state legislature. He was imprisoned in the famous fairgrounds stockade, where the police kept tape over their badge numbers to make it harder to file brutality reports. Two pregnant women lost babies after being beaten in the stockade. Ben accidentally dropped his plate into a tank of boiling water while passing through the food line; the guards forced him to reach in and get it out, and his hand was badly burned.

It was about this time that a Jackson policeman told him, "Someday, boy, I'm going to kill you."

Ben thought about going to college. But he was disturbed by the pull-out of SNCC and other northern-supported groups at a time when the need was growing, not lessening. He joined Delta Ministry's Freedom Corps—the freewheeling, gutsy group of young Negro men and women who helped organize the poor and register the voters in Delta towns that hadn't been reached before by the movement. Ben was run out of towns and chased off plantations at gunpoint.

Periodically broke (their subsistence pay was $10 a week, later raised to $20), the Freedom Corps ate at our house several times. On these occasions Ben would sit at the piano, playing the one tune he knew over and over, loudly, until persuaded—sometimes bodily—to stop.

When Delta Ministry began to run out of money and the Freedom Corps had to be disbanded, Ben went to Mount Beulah. The refugees from the air base, joined by families direct from the plantations, had come there to live—150 of them, mostly children.

Ben, a happy-go-lucky guy who stayed militant without letting it eat him up inside, got along well with the children at Mount Beulah. Like a bearded Pied Piper, he led them around the campus, telling stories, teaching them games. He told them about Negroes who had helped build America and had died for the movement. He even performed what some of us considered the most courageous act of the summer: single-handed, he took sixty kids on a field trip to the zoo.

When the land was finally purchased and the people moved from Mount Beulah up to the new Freedom City, Ben went to Jackson and got a job as a truck driver. The day before Christmas he married Margaret Willis, a beautiful girl from Natchez whom he'd met in the Freedom Corps.

He was discouraged by what he considered the failure of the Freedom Movement; the slow dwindling of Delta Ministry funds was another promise broken. He attended a few civil rights meetings, but concentrated mostly on his job and his marriage.

On May 10, 1967, two Jackson police drove onto the campus of Jackson State College, two blocks from Ben's apartment, to make a traffic arrest. This violated an agreement between the city and the college, which has its own security force. Students demanded that the policemen leave; the officers called for reinforcements and the disturbance escalated into a loud demonstration.

Lynch Street, a main thoroughfare that runs through the campus, was sealed off, and the students poured into the street. They burned the barricades and a phone booth and broke street lights.

The next night Mayor Thompson, whose main claim to fame is the $100,000 anti-riot "Thompson tank" he persuaded the city to buy, was ready for the students. Jackson city police, the state highway patrol, and the all-white national guard, with tanks and machine guns, moved into the campus area before dusk. Some students and about one hundred teen-agers gathered and responded with bottles and bricks.

(One hundred miles to the south, at the University of Southern Mississippi, a white institution, several *thousand* students were rioting. They threw bricks and bottles at police, blacked out the entire campus by cutting the power lines, and roughed up the dean. But instead of calling out the guard, officials called it a "typical spring panty raid," kept reporters away, and let it burn itself out.)

Ben's first cousin, an army private, was en route to Vietnam and was spending part of his leave with Ben and Margaret. He was in his uniform, walking from the downtown area to Ben's apartment, when a white national guard officer stopped him on Lynch Street. "What *you* doin' here, nigger?" the officer demanded.

Around 8 P.M., Ben walked from the house to the Kon-tiki, a cafe on Lynch Street, to get a sandwich for Margaret. He was with a friend, a medic just back from a year in Vietnam.

They found the Kon-tiki too crowded and started down Lynch Street toward the College Inn. "Then we heard shots," Ben's friend said later, "and we started running. I looked around, and Ben was lying on the ground."

The police, instead of using tear gas or shooting over the

students' heads, had deliberately fired into the retreating crowd.

One shotgun slug hit a Jackson State football player who had been standing at the window of his second-story dormitory room. Another hit a student who had been walking across the lawn, half a block away. A third blasted a sixteen-year-old boy who was among the demonstrators. Three slugs, of the kind you use to kill deer, hit Ben Brown from behind. One was in his leg, one lodged in his stomach, and the third went through the back of his neck and out his mouth.

As Ben lay motionless in the street, a group of students approached. The police waved them away. "But he needs help," one of the students said.

"He's got all the help he's ever gonna get," a cop shouted back.

Ben lay in a no man's land alone for ten minutes. A national guard medic climbed out of a tank and looked at him briefly. It was forty-five minutes before he was taken to University Hospital.

Ben Brown's funeral—Freedom Corp members are the pallbearers (*Robert Analavage*)

At 4:42 A.M., while Ben's mother, his wife, Margaret, and Delta Ministry friends from Mount Beulah waited outside the recovery room, Ben died.

Ben Brown was not a typical Delta Ministry staff member. In fact, there are very few who are typical. The people who have worked at various times under the title "Delta Ministry staff" surely compose one of the more wildly varied collections of mankind.

Their ages range from sixteen to eighty-three, and the average age at any given time has always been over thirty. Some have had doctorates, and some barely finished third grade. In faith they have represented the spectrum from Conservative Baptist to agnostic. Long before Vatican II nudged various ecumenical agencies into becoming interfaith as well as interchurch, the DM payroll included Jews, Roman Catholics, all kinds of Protestants, and one B'hai.

Approximately one hundred different names have appeared on payrolls at some time in the project's first three years, either as full National Council of Churches appointed staff, as NCC clerical workers, or as subsistence volunteers receiving only their basic living expenses. At least twenty-five more were long-term volunteers supported directly by churches or community organizations in the North.

The first five staff members were clergymen. But the hundred who followed included journalists, farmers, teachers, and factory hands.

Dan Smith, the economic development director, had been a nightclub operator. His predecessor, Al Winham, had spent thirty years as a parish minister. Nash Basom had worked for the poverty program; so had John Bradford and Curtis Hayes, in between stints as SNCC organizers. Clarence Hall and Jake Ayers worked in northern-owned Greenville factories, and both joined the staff after being fired for civil rights involvement. Owen Brooks was an electronics engineer. Thelma Barnes had been secretary to a Methodist bishop and to the president of a state college. Many of the staff left higher-paying jobs to join DM, but a few came off welfare.

Most of them had just two things in common: an obsession for seeing justice done in Mississippi and a history of civil rights activity back home where they came from.

None of them came trained for the specific job they did. There just isn't any training for that kind of thing. This job description—in the official jargon required by the office in New York—gives an idea of the things a staff member might be required to do:

## County Director—Delta Ministry Project

#### NATURE OF WORK

This is responsible and specialized work involving direction of the program of the Delta Ministry Project in a specific county or similar area in Mississippi. Work is performed with considerable independence under the general supervision of the director. Technical assistance will be available from program specialists. Supervision may be exercised over administrative or clerical assistants and volunteer workers.

#### EXAMPLES OF WORK PERFORMED

Develops and maintains effective relationships with the churches and residents of the county to enlist their cooperation and participation in the program. Similarly develops and maintains such relationships with civic, government and civil rights groups.

In consultation with the director and technical specialists, develops and carries out such programs as:

*Relief*—Locates sources of food and clothing and distributes to needy residents.
*Economic Development*—Assists in encouraging industries to locate in area to provide employment.
*Education*—Establishes programs in literacy training, remedial

and expanded liberal arts studies, vocational training, and
other appropriate educational projects.

*Health*—Develops private and public health resources for needy
residents.

*Citizenship*—Promotes concern for citizenship opportunities and
obligations.

*Culture*—Develops awareness of culture of the area and plans
programs of education in area and in exchange with other
areas.

*Community Centers*—Establishes and maintains center where
functions and activities of ministry are carried out, such
as arts and crafts, child day care, and recreation.

*Farm Program*—Develops program of producer and consumer
cooperatives in cooperation with indigenous farm programs.

Develops and maintains liaison with governmental personnel,
working with them in the adapting of federal programs
for the Delta area.

Administers budget for area.

Assigns, supervises and motivates subordinates, employed and
volunteer, in their work.

No two county directors go at this job the same way.
And, needless to say, no county director tries to do all the
things listed. The program ends up a different thing in each
county, because it is determined by two things: the needs
of the people in the county as they themselves see it and
the interests, skills, and available budget of the DM county
director.

Thus Sunflower County may concentrate on political
action, Issaquena on Head Start, and Washington County
on welfare services. A visitor who asks, "What is the Delta
Ministry doing today?" might have to be told, for example,
that on a given day Joe Harris was in a day-long meeting
with other officers of the Freedom Democratic Party,
Thelma Barnes was checking on the maladministration of
food stamps, Clarence Hall was trying to convince a young
farmer to run for constable, Harry Bowie was conducting a
workshop for black candidates for county office, and Roger

Smith and Earmia Jean Phillips were walking a picket line in Edwards.

This flexibility is part of the heritage of Art Thomas, DM's first director.

Art set the tone for the Delta Ministry as part of a *movement*. That means a good bit more than just being in favor of civil rights. It means being willing to operate as a full member of a vague, unorganized group for which there is no table of organization and no membership list. It means, for the Delta Ministry, paying the salaries of people whose main loyalty is to another organization—the FDP, the Poor Peoples' Conference, or the Mississippi Freedom Labor Union. It means being willing to commit money and time to a job for which somebody else will get all the credit, as in the case of Charles Evers' campaign for Congress.

The Church has talked for centuries about the need to lose itself in the concerns of others, but it has been pretty careful about seeing that it gets credit for its successes. Delta Ministry tried to break with that tradition.

Being part of the movement is a style of life, a way of looking at things in which the mystical "needs of the peoples" outweigh all organizational considerations.

This mode of operation often created tension with the NCC offices in New York. Filling out a job description and other NCC personnel papers seemed irrelevant to a person whose main interest in the NCC was that its money helped keep him in Mississippi. Even for those of us who knew and understood the demands of New York laws upon the business office, the papers often had pretty low priority when compared with the emergencies and crises demanding our time.

New York had to raise money to keep DM going, so it had to know what the project was accomplishing. DM said it wasn't accomplishing anything; the local peoples were doing it all with a little help here and there.

New York wanted to know how to justify keeping a man on the payroll whose mission in life was organizing local branches of the Freedom Democratic Party. New York wanted to know if DM's secretaries were observing the official state holidays, as required by the wage and hour laws; DM said nobody was about to take off on Robert E. Lee's birthday and Confederate Memorial Day—besides, most of the clerical staff worked seven days a week anyway.

Delta Ministry is officially a project of the Division of Christian Life and Mission, one of the NCC's four main divisions. Jon Regier, executive secretary of the division, is a shrewd, visionary gamecock of a man who formerly worked in Chicago's slums. He understands the nature of a movement, as does the NCC's general secretary, R. H. Edwin Espy. Both men have fought long and hard to keep DM alive and to keep it the kind of freewheeling operation it must be to do the job.

Many people visualize the life of a civil rights worker in Mississippi as a continual encounter with danger and death. But that isn't quite the case.

In the first place, Mississippi's officials were concerned enough about the state's image late in 1964 to put out the word that violence was no longer to be tolerated, at least until the challenge of the congressional delegation by the FDP had been settled. This had a dampening effect.

In the second place, those who were still working in the state by that time knew how to avoid most unnecessary danger. If you had to drive through Rolling Fork at night in an "integrated" car, you did so, but you didn't stop for gas. If you wanted to eat out with friends of a different color, you usually ate in Negro cafes; desegregation of public accommodations was pretty much irrelevant by then anyway.

Thus, when I once made a list of the physical hazards I had seen people incur through membership on the Delta Ministry staff, it came out like this:

*Cut fingers:* lacerated while stuffing newsletters into envelopes.

*Sore back:* from hours spent sorting boxes of clothing sent down from the North.

*Stomach pains:* from irregular eating habits and too much hot sauce, grits, Cokes, barbecue, and rice.

*Flat feet:* from canvassing door to door for eight to ten hours, urging people to register, vote, come to freedom rallies, or enroll their children in a formerly all-white school.

*Sore ear:* from spending five hours on the telephone, tracking down a missing volunteer or notifying staff members of a meeting.

There were exceptions to the rule of waning violence. Bob Fitzpatrick, a law student who had been following school buses in Issaquena County to see if they were segregated, was kicked and beaten unconscious in a store in Mayersville. He had two ribs broken, and the justice of the peace in whose store the beating occurred added insult by fining him $100 for driving recklessly near a school bus.

Bob Beech, DM's Hattiesburg director, bought something in a hardware store and, when the owner recognized Beech's name on the check, got punched in the nose. Beech took the man to court; after the jury acquitted him, he jumped Beech again in the lobby of the court house on the way out.

Shots were sometimes fired from the woods surrounding the Mount Beulah campus, and somebody once blew out Beech's front window with a shotgun blast just after he had left the room.

But those most likely to suffer violence in Mississippi

Bob Beech showing Warren McKenna what a shotgun blast did to his bedroom window (*Bruce Hilton*)

since fall 1964 have been the local black people. There is a cynical and realistic reason for this, one which indicts all the country. Mississippi's racial extremists learned, through the experiences of the 1964 summer, that the North was deeply concerned about the safety of the white "outside agitators" it sent down. The uproar over the deaths of Goodman, Chaney, and Schwerner in Neshoba County resulted as much from the fact that two of the victims were white as from the nature of the crime.

This theory was tested at Selma, where the death of James Reeb brought action which the equally outrageous murder of black Jimmie Lee Jackson a few days earlier had failed to trigger. It has been tested again with the deaths of Vernon Dahmer, Wharlest Jackson, Ben Brown, and others in Mississippi; none caused the stir which the death of young white Jonathan Daniels in Alabama did.

So it is no accident that since the end of 1964 there has

been no serious attempt on the life of a white civil rights worker or, for that matter, on any black outsider who has family and friends in the North to raise a fuss. The Klansmen recognize the racism of the North and use it.

The scars most civil rights workers bear from the battle in Mississippi are mental and emotional, rather than physical. Some have ulcers; some seem to live in a permanent state of irritability. A few who have been around for more than three years seem incapable of emotion, as though they have formed calluses against fear, hate, hope, and joy; their eyes are glazed, like the walking dead.

I once stayed awhile with a former SNCC worker who was helping DM; every morning, immediately after waking, he ran into the bathroom and threw up. One former DM staff member works only two or three days a week—enough to buy groceries—and spends the rest of the time incommunicado in his locked room.

It is not necessarily fear which leaves these scars. It might be any or all of these: official harassment, the knowledge of constant surveillance, the burden of a continual sense of outrage, or the tensions within the staff itself.

Police harassment is a fact of life for DM staff members. Officers of the law know how to make life miserable for a man. The police of Indianola used to follow DM's Sunflower County director, Joe Harris, every time he drove through that town, until on one such occasion a patrolman got confused and U-turned right into the side of another car.

Morgan Brown, delivering boxes of clothing for DM to distribution points in Bolivar County, was followed by Cleveland police one day until one of the boxes fell off his truck. He was jailed for "littering" and for "making an illegal stop" to pick up the box.

If you're the kind who gets a little uneasy and over-cautious every time a police car turns up behind you in the traffic, no matter how clear your conscience, you'll appreciate the tension generated by a hostile Mississippi cop following a DM staffer halfway across a county. This has happened to all the staff, not just once but often.

The Reverend James McRee, leader of the Madison County Freedom Movement and a member of the DM Commission, was followed by a state patrolman very late one night on a lonely stretch of highway. After a while the patrolman pulled into the left lane, alongside McRee's car and a little ahead of it, and turned his spotlight back so it shone directly into McRee's eyes. The two cars sped along like that for maybe two miles. And then the patrol car pulled on ahead and disappeared down the road.

Sometimes there's nothing to do but laugh at the way "law and order" is enforced. Rims Barber was once arrested for reckless driving while he was parked. And Owen Brooks was jailed for grand larceny after taking the Delta Ministry truck from in front of the Cleveland police station, where it had been left after an earlier driver was hauled in on a traffic charge. The larceny charge was later changed to an equally ridiculous one—trespassing.

The attitude of Mississippi's finest was demonstrated one night by a state patrolman who also added a new phrase to the DM vocabulary. He had been following the blue DM carryall, in which were riding four or five of the Freedom Corps members and a striking blond volunteer who was going from Mount Beulah to Greenville. Finally he stopped the car. After making each of the black men get out and submit to a search, with hands on top of the car, he told the lady to get out.

"These here boys are low enough," he spat out. "But for associating with them, you're lower than that. You're lower than whale dung, and that's at the bottom of the ocean."

The fact that the police, and a lot of other people, know exactly who you are and keep an eye on you is another effective weapon in the psychological battle. Your license plate is known to police all over the state, and your face to people all over the county.

Nash Basom and two visitors from the North attended a Klan rally east of Greenville (the one place in the state where they could have got away with it). They dressed as inconspicuously as possible, hoping they'd be considered just part of the crowd. But two strangers came up to Nash and called him by name. "You drove up from Jackson yesterday in a Volkswagen bus," one man said, "and these two men who are with you came up from Jackson the day before in a white Chevrolet." He was right on both counts.

Staff members know that the office phones are tapped and that from time to time their home phones are tapped, too. It's a common experience while carrying on a supposedly two-way private conversation to hear a third person cough.

It isn't so clear *who* taps the phones; it could be the Klan, the Citizens' Council, the state-financed Sovereignty Commission, the police, or the FBI. It wouldn't do much good to complain, as several of these groups have the cooperation of the phone company itself in making taps. The only defense is being careful what you say over the telephone.

Even the search for relaxation can turn out to produce stress instead. Where do you go for a good time, for example? Even if you're not in an interracial group that night, you avoid as a matter of principle the places known to be segregated. For those who drink, this rules out all the bars and nightclubs on the white side of town; as "private clubs" they remain segregated. You can go to the Negro Elks or VFW clubs, but if you're white you can't ever quite fit in; your skin gives you a high visibility, and in the current mood of black consciousness may even make you quite unwelcome.

You may go to a movie. This means deciding whether to give your principles a vacation and sit in the Jim Crow balcony, or insist that the group sit downstairs in the white section and suffer doubly: it costs twice as much, and your enjoyment of the movie is going to be interrupted by heckling and dirty looks.

Mostly for this reason, poker became the sole form of group entertainment for the DM staff in its first year. The games, with paper debts which sometimes climbed into the hundreds of dollars and usually went unpaid, lasted till three or four in the morning. There was no conversation outside the game—just deal the cards and get down to the bets. It was one way of getting out of Greenville for a few hours.

"You can't stay mad all the time," the cliché says. But in a sense the DM staff does. And this is bound to be still another drain on the emotions.

Every day, the staffer sees or learns about new injustices; these are added to the mountainous stockpile of inequities and outrages that already dominate his horizon. He can't just shrug them off, because they happen to people he knows intimately and represent defeats in the battle he's giving all his time and energy to.

He picks up the paper and sees that the FHA, whose county committee is trying to take away the farm of a Negro who dared to run for office in Mayersville, has made a loan of half a million dollars to planters in northern Mississippi to build a country club.

A staff member is jailed on a minor charge and it takes

seven hours to raise the $500 bail. Another staffer is informed he'll be cut from the payroll in three weeks because the money is running out.

A baby, suffering from malnutrition, is brought to the DM office. It dies in a staff member's arms. The mother says the hospital and welfare people turned her away.

Six weeks' work, on five hours' sleep a night, leads up to an election in which a Negro candidate has a chance to win for the first time in this century. And the plantation people, on their boss-men's direct orders, do not come in to vote. A racist stays in office.

Or the town of Utica, 65 percent black, re-elects its white mayor for four years. The only public filing notice was a three-by-five card tacked on the inside of the front door of the municipal office. By the time the local black movement learned about it, it was too late for another candidate to file.

If you're in the movement in Mississippi, you have your hopes dashed again and again by things like these. You live with a sense of the unfairness of things, of outrage at the apathy and greed and bureaucratic fumbling that make these things happen.

But the major source of ulcers and twitches is not the enemy. It's the people with whom you live and work, your closest friends.

Dr. Alvin F. Poussaint, a psychiatrist who was field director for the Medical Committee for Human Rights in Jackson for a while, wrote in *The New York Times Magazine*, August 20, 1967, that he used to sit and wonder, "Now, what do they really do with their rage?"

Well, after a period of time it became apparent that they were directing it mostly at each other and the white civil-rights workers. Violent verbal and sometimes physical fights often occurred among the workers on the civil-rights projects throughout the South.

While they were talking about being nonviolent and "loving" the sheriff that just hit them over the head, they rampaged around the project houses beating up each other. I frequently had to calm Negro civil-rights workers with large doses of tranquilizers for what I can describe clinically only as acute attacks of rage.

Although Dr. Poussaint interviewed and wrote about black workers for his article, the whites faced many of the same pressures. In fact, during the time described here, black people in the movement were moving toward a clearer and stronger appreciation of themselves, while the white workers found their role increasingly uncertain.

I know of only one fistfight between staff members of the Delta Ministry in its first three years. But staff meetings often were grim, painful occasions, dominated by the waves of hostility that washed back and forth. Lasting sometimes eight or ten hours, with visibility and available oxygen reduced to near zero by great clouds of cigarette smoke, and always dominated by the prospect of imminent bankruptcy, these staff meetings were for me the

Staff meeting in Greenville (*Toge Fujihira*)

worst single burden of life in Mississippi. All the pent-up frustrations each staffer felt about his work, the imperceptible gains, the apathy of the rest of the country, and the uncertain future of the whole project—all these frustrations seemed to be turned inward on the staff. We couldn't slug the mayor or the sheriff (even if it weren't a physically dangerous thing to do, we were bound by a rule of nonviolence); we couldn't vent our frustration on the local people; we ended up crucifying one another.

Misunderstandings were compounded by the wide variety in background and in needs, by occasional, severe black-white tensions, and by the necessity for each staffer to compete with the others, on behalf of his project, for the meager funds available.

Inability to find creative channels for this tension, to think as a staff, and to give one another badly needed support is, I think, the Delta Ministry's one biggest failure.

There are little defeats every day, of course, made inevitable by errors in judgment, the difficulty of long-range planning, countermoves by the segregationists, and the uphill nature of the whole fight. But DM's most honest critics agree that it has brought some hope to people who had no hope, it has identified with the poor in a unique way and made honest attempts to let them determine policy, and it has enabled the poor to bring pressure for important change on state, local, and national agencies.

The one group to which DM seems unable to minister is itself.

Early in the planning for DM, Art Thomas had written "A Proposal for a Common Discipline of the Delta Ministry Staff." The staff would come together regularly for worship and for study, he wrote, because before it could give of itself, it had to have something to give. In order to understand their role in a pioneer ministry, attempting to fulfill in a new kind of structure the "servant nature" the Church is supposed to have as Christ's body, they needed to discuss and study it. And in a culture where many of them were not welcome in churches of their own denomination, staff members would need the strength that comes from common worship.

This kind of study and worship happened only a few times. For one thing, after Art left, the temporary leadership on the field was hostile to any discussion of the Christian faith as a motivating force in DM.

But a more important reason, one which was felt even during Art's term of leadership, was the overreaction by the staff toward the white Church in Mississippi.

The churches, more fully described in the next chapter, dominate the political and social life of the community and even, with their huge air-conditioned sanctuaries, its architecture. Ministers are important men, and every public official and candidate for office must be noticeably pious. And the overwhelming majority of this influence the

Staff meeting—in the days when movement people still sang (*Bruce Hilton*)

Church holds is used in justifying and protecting the status quo.

A Delta Ministry staff member who hears a segregationist radio preacher asking the Lord's strength and guidance is understandably hesitant about suggesting to his fellow workers that they do the same. A militant young Negro who has been shoved down a flight of steps while attempting to enter a worship service tends to be cynical about the value of saying those same words and singing the same songs in another setting.

This doubt, this shame, this fear of being associated with something which so easily lends itself to distortion, meant that members of the DM staff pretty much kept their own council on matters of faith. There is no doubt that the love of Christ brought many of the staff to Mississippi and sustains them in the continual battle. But the help they might receive from one another in worship and in clarifying discussion of this faith just isn't available. Few of them like talking about it.

It would not be fair to the staff or to the project to end this chapter on such a negative note. The staff members are where they are by choice. Nearly every one of us who has left the staff has done so involuntarily. So it is obvious that there are compensations that outweigh the troubles.

Chief of these is being where the action is. Not many people, in this automated age, have the luxury of being on the scene and playing an important role in a work of obvious importance, one worth devoting one's self to body and soul, one where the battle lines are clearly drawn, one which makes possible a few real and identifiable victories now and then. Mississippi offers that luxury.

Another compensation is friendship. Common troubles, time together in jail or in danger, common enemies, and even the hot but honest battles of the staff meetings produce some deep friendships.

If the work in Mississippi produces some of the most miserable days in a man's life, it also provides some of the happiest, and certainly the most satisfying.

# 11. The Body of Christ

"*Since May of 1954, the sermons in most Southern churches have been concerned with the virtues of happiness and the evils of juvenile delinquency.*"
　　　　　—*Harry Golden*, MR. KENNEDY AND THE NEGROES

"*At first the deacons said 'no' to freedom rallies in our church. Then, when we decided to build a new church, they said okay. It didn't matter if the old one got burned down.*"
　　　　　—*Elder*, MOUNT PISGAH BAPTIST CHURCH

OUR VISITOR WAS EMBARRASSED.

"You know how glad I am you came to our church," the caller said. "There are several of us members who have welcomed you.

"But the pastor is in a very difficult position right now. Two of the biggest contributors to the building fund have said that if you and your family continue coming to our church, they will withdraw their pledges.

"You know how badly we need the new building. So the pastor thought—well, that if you understood the situation, you would see that it might be better if you stayed away for a while. At least until the building fund drive was over."

We didn't go back to the church. Or to any of the white churches of Greenville whose studied coolness made it clear we were not welcome. In the first eighteen months we lived in Greenville, we had made repeated visits to at least a half-dozen different white churches. Our first concern was to find a place of worship for the family; our second was to try to establish communication with the churchgoing whites of Greenville.

During each service we were given a visitor's card of some kind, and we always checked the box marked "Will the Pastor please call." No pastor ever came.

Eventually we realized that we had been naive to expect any other kind of welcome. For the white church is not just an example, a result, of segregation in Mississippi. It has been a major force in creating, justifying, and perpetuating the social structure that exists; it is the cornerstone of the closed society.

If you live in parts of the country where the Church is much less powerful and prestigious, you may have trouble understanding this. But sociologists at Mississippi State University learned that while the national average is one church for every 814 people, the Mississippi average is one church for every 289 people. A survey in Itawanba County reported that 73 percent of the adult population were church members and that 78 percent of these claimed they attended church at least three times a month. The number of ministers per capita in the Magnolia State is 66 percent above the New York average.

If you want to run for governor, mayor, or dogcatcher, you must be a church member, and preferably a deacon or Sunday school teacher (Ross Barnett taught Sunday school for years). The name plate under a portrait in the Old Capitol Museum in Jackson is engraved thus:

Julian Power Alexander, 1887–1953
Elder, First Presbyterian Church
U.S. District Attorney, 1919–1922

Associate Justice, Supreme Court of Mississippi, 1941–1953

The minister, while he has more prestige than power in a community, is part of every public function, pronouncing invocations and benedictions and lending the required air of piety. The power structure knows, too, that the minister, as a person who interprets "the Word," is a man they can use to sell an idea to the people.

Little of this prestige is exerted, so far, on the side of social justice. While their denominations made statements on racial justice years ago, the three white bishops in Mississippi (Roman Catholic, Methodist, and Episcopal) did not speak out on the issue until June 1, 1967. They broke their silence at that time to urge creation of a state biracial commission to discuss the race question—"hardly a startling or radical proposal," the *Delta Democrat-Times* said.

Meanwhile, in the school year which had just ended, at least fourteen private, segregated schools were operating in churches: five Baptist, five Methodist, and four Presbyterian.

Of the thousands of white churches in the state, there are not more than a dozen where a black man can present himself for worship without being physically—and often violently—barred from entering.

This support of the status quo affected the churches' attitude toward the Delta Ministry, beginning long before the staff arrived.

Fair warning of this attitude was given as early as July 1963. It was then that a delegation of five white ministers, representing the National Council of Churches, visited Clarksdale, Mississippi.

Ministers and lay representatives of Clarksdale's white churches refused to see them. The churches of St. Andrew's Presbytery in northern Mississippi cut off financial support to the NCC. And shortly afterward a large association of Methodist laymen and ministers announced they would sue the NCC and various civil rights groups for causing a "drop in membership, loss of financial support . . . mental suffering and fear on the part of a majority of Mississippi Methodists." (Chairman of the legal advisory committee was John C. Satterfield, a former president of the American Bar Association and a perennial delegate to his denomination's General Conference.)

It went downhill from there. By March 1964—six months before the first staff member was on the job for Delta Ministry—two apostles of the radical right were making speeches (and taking collections) in Mississippi churches; both Dr. Carl McIntire of the tiny American Council of Churches and W. G. Lowman of the Circuit Riders were denouncing the yet unborn Delta Ministry. McIntire's message was entitled "Revolution in the Delta," and his newspaper ads promised: "National Council of Churches to Invade Mississippi With Agrarian Reform Revolution." "The NCC Has Voted to Invade Mississippi." "Your Church Money Might Be Used in Socializing America."

The response of the North Mississippi Conference of the Methodist Church was to adopt a motion permitting churches to cut off funds to the National Council. Galloway Church, the largest Methodist congregation in the state, dropped its $6700 contribution forthwith.

With this kind of advance billing, it was no wonder that when DM actually arrived on the scene it had trouble with the white churches. Afraid to talk to us, and thus without access to reliable information on our work, they could see little of the good we were doing. The terrific pressures put on pastors by their laymen and in turn by pastors on area administrators caused a two-pronged reaction: loud efforts by the pastors to dissociate themselves from us and concerted efforts to run us out of the state.

Leaders of the Mississippi convention of the Christian Church (Disciples of Christ) fought bitterly to keep DM from leasing Mount Beulah. They told denomination officials in Indianapolis that the whole Mississippi convention would withdraw from the church if DM got Mount Beulah. When the denomination went ahead with the lease, the Mississippi churchmen instituted a scorched-earth policy at Mount Beulah, urging maintenance employees to take away anything that wasn't nailed down. Cleaning equipment, ladders, tools—all were removed. The kitchen was stripped of utensils and equipment. Even the light bulbs were removed or broken.

The Disciples weren't the only ones who tried the denominational end run. The Reverend John A. Allin, bishop coadjutor of the Episcopal Church in Mississippi, was instrumental in getting the executive council of his denomination to pass a reasonable-sounding resolution in December 1964, just three months after DM began. The council had okayed a national appeal for $100,000 for race relations projects, including DM; Bishop Allin's amendment stated that if priests of the Episcopal Church were engaged in any projects for which these funds were to be used, the consent of the local bishop must be obtained. It sounded innocent enough.

But it meant that DM stood to lose the services of the Reverend Warren McKenna and the Reverend H. J. Bowie, both Episcopal priests; their chances of getting Bishop Allin's approval to work in his state were only slightly better than those of, say, Generals Sherman and Grant. Warren had been administrator of the program to bring minister-counsellors into the state to work with the COFO volunteers during the preceding summer; his contacts, his knowledge of Mississippi, and his cool, dry approach to continual crisis made him irreplaceable. Bowie, a Negro from the New Jersey diocese, was to plan and lead the successful citizenship education programs for DM, training and recruiting both voters and candidates.

Fortunately, when they discovered what was going on, the clergy of the church made such a racket that the executive council rescinded the order at its February 1965 meeting.

One group used the denominational end run approach to hit DM where it really hurt: its hopes of easing hunger in the Delta. This paragraph from the DM Executive Committee minutes of July 19, 1965, tells that story:

> We have tried to secure program cooperation from Church World Service of the NCC. CWS had hoped to modify their policy and to become involved in direct domestic relief rather than only overseas relief, but this has not happened.
>
> One of the problems regarding our relationship with CWS is that one of their constituent groups, an entire denomination, has stated that none of their funds for CWS should go to any project having anything to do with civil rights.
>
> To continue working with us would force this denomination out of Church World Service.

But no national group felt more pressure against participating in DM than the Methodist Board of Missions. Methodism's southern churches, which had just patched up a Civil War schism with the northern churches in 1939, continually threatened to split off again. They were powerful, wealthy and vociferous. They did not want DM in Mississippi, and they did not want denominational mission board funds, much of which they had contributed, to go to "civil rights" work.

At the same time, some northern churches and a small but determined and dedicated group of mission board staff members were working in favor of Methodist participation.

Two years went by while this battle in the board's New York headquarters continued; DM had hoped for $100,000 a year from the Methodists, and its budget went into the red $180,000 during those two years. Finally, late in 1966, the board made a first annual grant of $70,000.

There were many people who fought for this decision, but two who earned a place in the hearts of the DM staff members were Miss Thelma Stevens and Miss Peggy Billings, of the board's Women's Division. Tirelessly dedicated to the idea that the board must back projects which were right, regardless of the consequences, these two ladies spoke with special power in answering the charges of the white Mississippians—because both of them were also white Mississippians born and bred.

In Mississippi, meanwhile, the churches continued to fight.

Much of the opposition was more direct, and apparently stemmed from the fear of guilt by association. Three times Roman Catholic priests came to Mississippi as volunteers for DM; each time, as custom requires, the volunteer made a courtesy call on the bishop in Jackson, and each time he was promptly sent home.

Even the new ecumenical spirit of Vatican II worked against us. Fred Lowry was warmly received at the diocesan chancery office late in 1966, but was told that the Catholics could have no public dealings with DM—"because we don't want to endanger our relations with the Methodists here."

A clergyman in Greenville managed to convince Bishop Moore, on one of our chairman's frequent peacemaking visits, that he was the only minister in town who really understood and supported the Delta Ministry. He assured the bishop of his quiet but firm support.

But within a week, in a speech to a small-town Rotary

club, he had attacked Delta Ministry as "incompetent and not really Christian in its approach." He praised the NAACP and described DM as a "way out group." When asked what qualifications DM staffers had for their jobs, he answered, "My answer, sir, is very simple. None."

The churches are afraid of association with DM even in the most innocent of activities. The United Presbyterian Church in the U.S.A. (the "Northern" Presbyterian churches in Mississippi) refused, after several weeks of debate, to let DM use their camp for a weekend staff retreat. And letters to state officials of all the denominations, offering to meet with them individually to answer questions about DM, went unanswered until 1967.

A couple of months after DM opened the Greenville office, the staff got the local white ministerial association to agree to a joint meeting. But when the YMCA learned that it would be an interracial meeting, it refused the ministers their usual meeting room in the "Y." And when the meeting was shifted to the DM office, only two ministers showed up.

Why are the churches so frightened, not just of DM, but of all open evidences of social change? The reasons pile up like bricks in a wall.

*First, Church leaders are people.* The deacons, elders, and moderators who make local church policy are also businessmen, plantation owners, politicians, gin operators, and fertilizer salesmen. Anything which threatens the plantation system, based on exploitation of the poor, threatens their income, their way of life. They are subject, not just to the commands of Christ, but to community pressure, social custom, family mores, and (in many areas) a continual flow of misinformation in the press.

Three northern ministers visited Mississippi in March

1964 to learn about the situation and understand the pressures on the Church there. Their report, written for the *Christian Advocate*, was largely sympathetic to the plight of the white pastor. It contained these observations:

> There is a conviction among the white citizenry that both colored and white persons made a good adjustment from slavery to a paternalistic relationship after the Civil War. In the light of this, the Supreme Court decision of 1954 looms as a horrible mistake by men who were either diabolically evil or unbelievably unenlightened. . . .
>
> There is a common assumption that the nation will sooner or later wake up and repudiate the Supreme Court decision.
>
> It appears that a majority of white Methodists in Mississippi would favor withdrawing from the Methodist Church before they would worship with Negroes on an equal basis.

Three years later, that still appears to be a statement of fact in Mississippi.

*Second, the Church is a social institution.* Making a church racially inclusive has for many southerners the same connotation as taking Negroes into one's home as social equals. And as a social institution the Church tends to reflect—rather than affect—the attitudes of its members.

Harry Golden, in *Mr. Kennedy and the Negroes* (New York, 1964), thinks this state of affairs results from the rise of a southern middle class in the last forty years:

> As the middle class proliferated, their need for self-expression also grew. . . . The well-off layman found he could fulfill his hunger for expression by managing his church. He along with others like him gave the church money, and then they formed a church committee and decided jointly how they would spend it. Eventually, too, this committee began to oversee the content of the Sunday sermon since they wanted their church to reflect them, not their minister who was now but an agent.
>
> When the race issue began intruding on Southern life, the middle-class deacons, stewards, elders and trustees told their clergymen, "Stick to religion."

As a result, the Protestant church throughout the South is rarely the champion of the unpopular cause, not even the unpopular cause remote from the racial crucible. The church conforms in almost all respects to the prevailing beliefs and sentiments of the overpowering majority.

*Third, Church leaders fear a strong stand would destroy their institutions.* Many churchmen do recognize that racial injustice is unchristian, but feel the Church must go very slowly in attacking it. They know that if they take an unpopular stand, the missions offerings, the building fund, even the membership of the Church itself will dwindle. They conclude they must forego one form of Christian witness—social action—in order to strengthen others—evangelism and missions.

Related to this is the feeling of the pastor who knows that if he "gets involved" in racial matters, or even gets the reputation of being soft on integration, he may split the congregation.

The tradition of congregational autonomy practiced by Southern Baptists—the largest denomination in Mississippi—means a clergyman is hired or fired at the will of the local congregation. The Methodists and Episcopalians have a system of pastoral appointment by bishops, which should provide a strong backstop for a man in a controversial situation; unfortunately, the result is usually the same in either case. The fear of a royal battle between those who favor the pastor and those who oppose him results in his removal "for the church's good."

This makes a man think long and hard before he speaks out clearly on social issues. "If I push too hard," he reasons, "I will have to leave, and can be of no more use to the congregation. If I go slow, I can stay and try to provide leadership for gradual change." Too often he finds, though, that any move whatsoever to change *what is* to *what ought*

*to be* is too much for his congregation; he ends up swallow-
ing his conscience and his tongue.

*Fourth, there is distrust for anything ecumenical, and
especially for the National Council of Churches.* The
Southern Baptist pattern, with its emphasis on the autonomy of the congregation, may be the foundation of distrust
for any movement which tends to unite the churches.
There is no state council of churches and not one local
council of churches in Mississippi. But this pattern also
stems from distrust of the NCC, going back at least twenty-
five years, to an earlier group, the Federal Council of
Churches.

The NCC and its predecessors have taken a strong public
stand on such issues as race and the right to organize unions.
Those who make their living preaching in tracts or on the
air against the NCC have operated most successfully in the
South where these two issues generally evoke negative re-
sponses.

*The fifth and most important reason for the white
churches' distrust of DM is theological; they don't believe
that what DM is doing is the Church's business.* This really
began to come home to me during the visit of a Presbyterian pastor from Cleveland, Mississippi—one of the few
white clergymen in the state who bothered to visit our
projects.

This pastor, whose colonial brick church and Christian
education building are worth over a million dollars, is, by
Mississippi standards, liberal. He is not afraid to use the
phrase "social action" in a sermon, or to follow up the
admonition to love mankind with an occasional reminder
that this means Negroes.

But as we drove the back roads, seeing the Delta Ministry men at work, he repeated again and again his con-

viction, "I'll admit much of this work needs to be done. But, Bruce, it is not the work of the Church."

On the last evening of his visit, we stood just after sundown in the mud of Strike City, talking with the strikers. He had spent half an hour with Mr. Green, John Henry Sylvester, and others, hearing them tell about life on the plantations. They were more comfortable in these tents, they said, than they had ever been in the tumble-down shacks they'd been evicted from. They told of sick babies who had had no doctor, and of being charged a dollar by the boss-man to ride into town to get their free government commodities. "We're still poor," Mr. Sylvester had said to the visiting pastor, "but we're not slaves any more. We work hard, but we work for ourselves."

I couldn't resist asking the visitor, as we walked back to the car in the dark, "You say that what we're doing here isn't the work of the Church. Tell me, what would *you* have done for these men when they were on the plantation?"

"That's simple," he said at once. "I'd build a chapel out here and win these folks for the Lord."

I didn't bother to argue the fact that for a variety of reasons "these folks" knew the Lord better than most of his parishioners did. Instead, I was churning over in my mind the realization that the Church's inability to help Mississippi is not just a response to social pressure, but stems from the southerner's *basic belief about the nature of the Church*. This intelligent and relatively open man could accept the Church's failure in social action because he really didn't think it belonged there in the first place.

Churchmen also complained that they had expected the Delta Ministry to "reconcile the races" and that instead it seemed to cause more bitterness, disagreement, and hatred than before.

Bishop Pendergrass, who twice flew to New York to speak against any funding of the Delta Ministry by the Methodist Board of Missions, circulated a paper which accused DM of fomenting "fear, suspicion and open animosity." The Bishop wrote that "local denominational leaders in Mississippi, both white and Negro, are unanimous in their opinion that the Delta Ministry program has widened the breach between the races."

His attempt to enroll Negro witnesses for his case fell apart in his second New York appearance when Bishop Golden—leader of Mississippi's black churches—stood to oppose him and to urge the mission board to support DM. But there is no use denying that during DM's early years, tensions between the races became much more apparent. The Greenville Mills picketing, the Andrews plantation strike, the air base incident, and other controversial events certainly caused new expressions of animosity—at least among whites.

DM would argue, of course, that the feelings had been there all along. Whites were only beginning to realize this gulf existed, because blacks were only just beginning to express their own true feelings in a way the whites could understand. And before reconciliation is possible, the staff would argue, the true nature of the schism, in all its vastness, has to be seen.

But the argument over whether a gap existed before the days of the Freedom Movement is not really the basic one. The real argument between organizations like the Delta Ministry (whether in Mississippi or in Watts) and their critics is over the basic nature of reconciliation.

To most whites, "reconciliation" conjures up pictures of a pleasant group of black men and white men sitting down around a table together, shaking hands and talking over mutual problems in a "reasonable" manner.

As a matter of fact, the Methodist Church in Mississippi

had set up just such a series of meetings in the early 1960s. But the black participants told a group of visiting northerners in 1964 that the meetings had been meaningless. Until they met as equals, they said, there was no real meeting at all.

The Delta Ministry staff—and most modern theologians—would argue that true reconciliation is possible only between men who regard each other as equals. As long as the servant-master or planter-tenant mentality exists between white men and black in Mississippi, reconciliation is an impossible dream.

The apostle Paul seemed to be recognizing this fact when he wrote his friend Philemon, hoping for a reconciliation between Philemon and the runaway slave, Onesimus. "Perhaps this is why he was parted from you for a while, that you might have him back forever, no longer as a slave, but more than a slave, as a beloved brother. . . ."

Thus, helping black people break the job barrier is a step toward reconciliation. So were the classes conducted by Harry Bowie of the DM staff and Lawrence Guyot of FDP for the black candidates in the 1967 elections, teaching them how to run a good campaign.

The successful boycotts in Shelby and in Edwards, in which Delta Ministry staff members helped support local leaders, forced the white power structure to deal with black citizens—for the first time in a century—as human beings.

This is why many of us believe that "black power"—despite some abuses—is the real force toward reconciliation of the races in America today. Black Americans are discovering, as did black Mississippians, that only when they use their power do whites accord them the respect which is a prerequisite of true reconciliation.

The picture I've given of the white churches, as choosing either active opposition or silence on social change, is generally true. But there are a few signs of change.

The statement of the three bishops on June 1, 1967, was one sign, although the *Democrat-Times* pointed out that "it was couched in generalities, and it came years later than it should have." The fact that it was made at all was significant.

The Mississippi Methodist Ministry, a mission to the poor of Clarksdale, is staffed by the two perceptive and able Killingsworth sisters, who spent most of their adult lives as missionaries in Malaya. When they found that they could not effectively work with the Negro community while living in the white community, they affiliated with the Central Jurisdiction (the Negro Methodists) and moved into the Negro section of Clarksdale. Their valuable work is still financed in part by the white Methodist conferences.

The Southern Baptists have set up half a dozen small "seminaries" for Negro pastors, few of whom have a high school education. And although many Negro clergymen charge that the schools teach the old philosophy of "be content with your lot—there's a pie in the sky by and by," the original intent seems to have been good.

And while the Baptists refused to desegregate Mississippi College in Jackson, their William Carey College in Hattiesburg has been integrated for several years.

Roman Catholic priests have stuck out their necks, too. When the record for the civil rights workers' stay in Yazoo City was three days because of harassment of the workers and their landlords by police, a Catholic priest let members of Delta Ministry's Freedom Corps sleep in his basement for three weeks.

St. James Episcopal Church in Greenville has received Negro visitors, as have a handful of Lutheran and Methodist churches around the state.

The Cleveland District clergy of the Methodist Church

finally came through with an invitation to talk about DM—a real break, considering that their superintendent had always refused to answer our letters. (However, the place of meeting had to be moved from First Methodist Church in Cleveland to the Wesley Foundation House at Delta State College because I had asked that Thelma Barnes and Solomon Gort join in the presentation—and an integrated meeting was impossible in the church.)

The churches and synagogues of the state cooperated in setting up a Committee of Concern, to rebuild churches which had been burned or bombed. Unfortunately, the committee's funds ran out before the arsonists' zeal did. But for clergymen to ally themselves publicly with even so "safe" a cause took courage and was a step forward.

Since the national Methodist Church began appropriating money to the Delta Ministry, the state leadership has made more effort to interpret our work to pastors and laymen. And the social action committee of a church in Columbus, Mississippi, 150 miles away on the other side of the state, drove to Greenville to visit the DM office and talk with staff members.

A small interracial group of clergymen has been meeting for three years in a Jackson restaurant every Thursday morning. And while the downtown Methodist church in Greenville was passing a resolution to exclude civil rights workers and Negroes, the pastor of another Methodist church became the first white clergyman ever to call in our home; his warm invitation and the reserved but not hostile reaction to our presence in his congregation afforded our family a place to worship the last six months we were in Mississippi.

One of the most hopeful signs for the Church in Mississippi has to be the United Church Women. Once a large, important, socially acceptable organization, the Mississippi

UCW blew up in 1964 when the national convention encouraged all groups to study race relations and passed a resolution banning discrimination in membership. When the dust settled, only a handful of women still belonged to the group in Mississippi. But this group of courageous women were of the kind that make things happen. (Jane Schutt, the president, had a bomb thrown on her front porch—a sign of relevance granted to few other women's groups anywhere in the country!) The DM staff was invited to the state convention—a gathering of about thirty women, half of them white. The state group's endorsement of a national Church Women project to provide a nurse at Freedom City was the first official approval by *any* Church body in Mississippi of *any* Delta Ministry program.

So there has been change. It is important to recognize this—but it is also important not to overestimate the change. In proportion to the numbers of churches, pastors, and members who still favor the status quo, it is very little change indeed. And what change has been made has been costly.

Individual pastors who have taken a public stand for real social change have had to suffer. Nobody can give an accurate count of the number of men who have had to leave the state. One Methodist conference alone lost sixty-eight pastors over this issue in nine years. Of the twenty-eight young pastors who in January 1963 issued a "Born of Conviction" statement through the Mississippi *Methodist Advocate*, only seven are still preaching in Mississippi. Their statement merely reaffirmed their belief in the brotherhood of man and in their right to free speech in the pulpit.

Perhaps most hated of the state's white ministers is the Reverend Edwin King, who was an active supporter of the

Freedom Movement from the very first. A native Mississippian, he became unwelcome in relatives' homes, was threatened with death, and was eventually (by a close vote) evicted from his annual conference.

He worked with the original SNCC and the Freedom Democratic Party (and drew 90,000 votes for lieutenant governor in the Freedom Vote of 1964). Arrested too many times to count, he has worked on a road gang and once escaped death from a lynching party only because a foreigner was in his car. Once he was beaten on the main street of downtown Jackson.

In September 1967 he joined the Delta Ministry staff as education director—the first white Mississippian DM had been able to recruit.

The list of clergymen whose courage has cost them their jobs includes two pastors of the state's largest and most prestigious church, Galloway Methodist. This congregation's vast building occupies a full block facing the state capitol, and the membership includes much of Jackson's leadership.

Dr. W. B. Selah, who had been pastor at Galloway eighteen years, supported the "Born of Conviction" statement, and resigned in protest when Negroes were turned away from the church by ushers acting under instruction from the official board. His successor, Jeff Cunningham, whose family included old-line Jackson aristocracy, was eased out as pastor because he tried quietly to achieve the same thing: an open church. (Bishop Gerald Kennedy spoke at Lenten services at Galloway in 1966, but insisted that Negroes be admitted. They were—but on the next Sunday members of the official board turned away a Negro woman who came to worship.)

The first guest I ever showed around the Delta was the Reverend Donald Thompson, who also was to pay a heavy price for his outspoken stands. Pastor of a small interracial Unitarian church in downtown Jackson, Mr. Thompson was a quiet, sensitive man who was as brave as he was big— and he was a big man.

One evening shortly after his visit to the Delta, he was shot down near his home in Jackson by a gun fired from a passing car, gangland style. Only his bulk, doctors said, kept the slugs in his neck and shoulder from killing him.

After a long convalescence in Boston, Thompson returned to Jackson to find that his parishioners were afraid to be seen with him. It took only a few days to find that he would have no support at all from the city's moderates. After several death threats, he quietly slipped out of town at 5:30 on a Monday morning, never to come back. He now works in Boston, in the job once held by another victim of hate, James Reeb.

Two years later, I was with the Reverend Bruce Nicholas when he got word that he, too, was a casualty. Bruce, a wiry, intense young man with a face lined and hair grayed far beyond his years, had been a controversial figure in Shelby for three years. Pastor of the Methodist church there, he had been trying to get the white men who held power—some of them members of his church—to meet with the real Negro leadership of Bolivar County. "Your hand-picked Uncle Toms tell you exactly what you want to know," he told county officials. "You'd better start to talk to real people."

As we sat in his living room waiting for word from the bishop, he chain-smoked and talked quietly about the last two years. He had learned to know leaders of the movement in Bolivar County. He had been in their homes, and he had persuaded some of his powerful white friends to go along on later visits (unprecedented in Bolivar County, where blacks come to whites, not vice versa). And he had pushed hard for full representation of the poor on the various programs funded by the Office of Economic Opportunity.

But meanwhile he was losing his congregation. Rumors flew that he was a "nigger-lover," that he planned to integrate the church, that he was a Communist. Town police began following his teen-age son wherever he drove. His phone was tapped.

Some of his more vociferous opponents demanded that he leave. They said the reason wasn't race, of course; they weren't prejudiced. No, it was that he was "neglecting his duties as a pastor," he "wasn't calling on the sick," he was "mixing in politics rather than preaching the gospel."

A student from Ole Miss conducted a survey that showed slightly more than half the members in favor of Bruce's ministry. His opponents ran their own survey, showing that slightly *less* than half favored Bruce. Finally the pastoral relations committee voted to ask the bishop for a new pastor.

The committee had been called to Jackson that morning to meet the bishop and was due back soon. One member of the committee—"one of the two persons in the whole church who are now with me"—was to report on the meeting as soon as they returned.

"The bishop will back me up," Bruce said. "He said he would. After all, this is 1967, not 1964. And if he does, I'll stay. If he doesn't, I'll have to leave the pastorate for a few years. After all, where can I go? Who'll have me?"

He had been offered a regional job with the anti-poverty program, he said, and wanted to stay in Shelby. "But I've checked, and nobody will sell me or rent me a house anywhere in this town."

Finally the doorbell rang. The friendly member of the pastoral relations committee came in. There were introductions all around, and we began to make small talk.

But Bruce broke in. "What did the bishop say? Will he stand by me?"

"Well," the man began, "he told us right away that the day is past when a congregation can get rid of its minister just because people don't like his views on the race issue."

There was a long pause. Finally Bruce asked, "But what did he say about this situation, here and now, in Shelby?"

The visitor looked down at the carpet. "Well, he said he realized that a lot of tension had been caused. He said he would have to do what was best for the church."

The tired face relaxed. Bruce stubbed out his cigarette and sagged back in the chair. "Well," he said, "that's a phrase I've heard before. And I guess we all know what it means. Thanks, though," he said as the visitor got up to leave. "Thanks for trying."

So far we've talked about the white church. What about the Negro church in Mississippi?

The problems faced by the congregation of St. John's Missionary Baptist Church, far off the main highway in rural Issaquena County, might help in understanding the situation.

Issaquena is almost entirely rural; its county seat, Mayersville, has only 150 residents. There is no doctor and no nurse in the county; there is a grade school but no high school.

To get to St. John's Church, you drive west from Glen Allan eight or ten miles, on a road that degenerates from tar to gravel to just plain dirt. You wind through cypress hollows, across flat, endless fields of cotton, between rows of rotting tenant shacks. And suddenly, as you round the bend, you see the church.

The congregation of this church was divided in the spring of 1965. Some of the deacons, including Clarence Hall, wanted the church used as a Head Start center. Others, re-membering that ninety-three churches had already been burned in the South in the last few years for civil rights activities, were against it. After all, they argued, this church was the only thing some of the members could call their own. They had squeezed pennies to build it and keep it up. It was not right, they argued, to risk losing it, even for a good project.

But those who wanted the center won. After all, the preparation for first grade could make all the difference in their children's futures. Besides, the salaries some of the mothers could earn as helpers and teacher trainees would be far beyond the three dollars a day they earned chopping cotton.

Once the decision was made, attendance at the church began dropping. The reason wasn't that people disagreed so violently. It was self-preservation. Most of them lived on plantations, and the boss-man knew that St. John's was going to be one of those "Freedom Rider" churches. There were enough people being told to leave the plantation any-way; a thing like this could get you your walking papers in a hurry.

By the time folks had the church fixed up to qualify as a Head Start center, the Sunday congregations had dwindled to less than half.

The center opened on a Monday morning. Around 2 A.M. on the following Thursday, the church somehow caught fire and burned to the ground.

When you drive out there now, you can see the cement front steps, leading to nowhere. Behind them, a partially melted kitchen stove and little piles of nails, hinges, and metal fittings are all you can find among the weeds.

But thirty yards away, on a new plot of ground, stands a new brick church. "Fireproof," the members tell you proudly. "Even the window frames are steel." There was some money from a special fund Drew Pearson has, and a little through the Delta Ministry, they said, but most of it they raised themselves.

Under conditions like this, the Negro church in Mississippi has all the troubles you might expect—and a few you wouldn't expect.

The Negro people are poor, with a median annual income across the state of less than a third of the white man's, and their churches reflect it. In order to survive, most pastors serve four churches in rotation, and hold a part-time job during the week. Many of the town pastors solicit white businessmen for contributions—a practice that has its effect on the militancy a pastor can be expected to show.

And the clergymen are poorly prepared. You can count the seminary-trained Negro pastors in Mississippi on your ten fingers. The Negro pastors tend to have the same theological tunnel vision as the southern white pastors; they also can be heard to say, "A preacher should stick to the gospel, and not get involved in all that social action stuff." In slavery days, the most valuable function the slave church filled was in keeping the people content; the reward for suffering would come in the next life.

The tendency to rationalize and excuse the inexcusable in society is still there. At the funeral of Ben Brown, a Negro clergyman referred several times to the fact that "the Lord has called our brother home." But the succeeding speaker rather bluntly disagreed: "The Lord didn't call our brother home. White cops murdered him. And it has come time to distinguish the difference."

Finally the first clergyman got up again. "How long," he asked, "will the Lord allow the white man to abuse our people this way?"

A former Mississippian, an A.M.E. pastor in Denver, told

Freedom rally—mixing the spirit of revivals and revolution (*Ken Thompson*)

me, "When I graduated from seminary, I went back to Mississippi, and they gave me a plantation church out near Leland. The second day I was there, the boss-man called me in. He handed me a ten-dollar bill and said, 'Your job is to keep my niggers happy. Do that, and I'll keep you happy.'

"I packed up," he said, "and left Mississippi the next day."

Most of the rural churches in the Delta are plantation churches. They are built by the planter for "his nigras"; he picks the preacher (often a foreman on the plantation) and decides what meetings can or cannot be held in the building.

This is a powerful force in the whites' control over the field hands. In many areas of the Delta, there is no other building available for such meetings as PTA, FDP, or a voter-registration rally. I know of one planter who refused to allow a traveling nurse to hold health meetings in the church on his land because he figured (quite rightly) that if his employeees had a chance to congregate outside the rigidly structured morning worship service, they might begin to plan jointly to change their economic situation.

The startling thing about the Negro church in Mississippi, however, is not the timidity or conformity, but the large number who have, like the members of St. John's Church, risked everything. The freedom rallies still take place in churches. Preachers with guts still play key roles in local movements. Of six FDP candidates for Congress in the fall of 1966, four were ministers of the Methodist Church.

The Reverend Clint Collier, one of those men, was beaten repeatedly during his campaign by whites in Neshoba County; he was daily followed along the back roads by Sheriff Rainey or his deputy, Cecil Price. The Reverend James McRee, another Central Jurisdiction Methodist, led an effective boycott of Canton, Mississippi, and made his church available as headquarters for the Meredith March when it came through his county.

Day in and day out across Mississippi, "the preacher" is risking his congregation's future and his tiny income to help register voters, organize workers, or train citizens.

The planter originally introduced "Christianity" to his "heathen" slaves to provide them with an emotional outlet and a means of escape—with religion's promise of eventual redress—from the oppression, boredom, and trouble.

There is not much difference between him and the twentieth-century planter who builds a church and pays a preacher to "keep my niggers happy." And there is not much difference between that modern planter and the bank president, deacon of First Church, who insists that if the pastor speaks out on the race issue, it must be to defend the status quo.

If there literally is one unforgivable sin, surely it must be the use of Christ's body, his Church, to deny fullness of life to people.

The preacher, under indictment for the murder of Vernon Dahmer and pronouncing the benediction at a rally of the White Knights of the Ku Klux Klan, is no more a violator of Scripture than the respectable minister of a million-dollar church who avoids comment on racial injustice because to do so would endanger the building program.

Eventually more churchmen in Mississippi must ask themselves: Is unity more important to the Church than being right? What does it do to a church to sacrifice its integrity to gain peace? What does it do to a man's soul to continue practicing, for whatever reason, what he knows is wrong?

# 12. Whole World in His Hands

"*The Church must prick the conscience of the West before the Third World bursts out in righteous indignation with acts of violence which, by comparison, would reduce the recent outbreaks in the U.S.A. to insignificance.*"

—LETTER TO WORLD COUNCIL OF CHURCHES FROM AFRICAN CHURCHMEN'S CONFERENCE

THERE IS A LADY who lives in the Delta, a long-time leader of the movement, who—no matter how often she's been beaten or jailed—has never been forced to cry. But when I told her, at a time when the need was most critical, that the Christian Council of India had sent $211 to help the poor of the Delta, then the lady cried.

The gift from India was just one of many signs that the rest of the world is interested in the black man's struggle for justice in America, and that churchmen around the world are interested in the Delta Ministry.

The idea of support from overseas, originally planned as just a gesture, became a source of funds which literally kept DM from folding. Since 1964 the overseas churches have given more than $300,000 to DM. The money comes through Interchurch Aid, an agency of the World Council of Churches, which lists more than six hundred projects to which world churches may send funds. DM is the first and only North American project on the list.

The gifts have included more than $60,000 from the British Council of Churches and more than $100,000 from "Bread for the World," a German church relief agency. They also include $280 from the Christian Council of South Africa (the English-speaking, integrated council there) and $100 a year from the Presbyterian Church in Cameroon. The East Asia Christian Conference contributed $2500 and the Netherlands around $100,000. Other gifts came from France, Australia, New Zealand, Canada, Finland, and Denmark.

Visitors came to the Delta from many of these countries, and there have been at least a dozen long-term volunteers (a month or more) from overseas. The experience was often a shock—an antidote to the image of America as a wealthy nation. Miss Janet Lacey, head of Britain's overseas relief organization, Christian Aid, spent ten days in the Delta with us; although she has visited most places of great need in the world, she called the Delta visit "the most shattering of my life."

The reason, she told reporters, that this bothered her more than even Calcutta, India, or Recife, Brazil, was that the misery in the Delta was a result "of the cruelty and stupidity of ordinary people who persecute others not only because they have different colored skin, but because they have different ideas."

A network television team from Holland produced a one-hour documentary on the Delta Ministry which was shown in that country on Christmas Day 1966, and then repeated two months later by viewer request.

All this interest, of course, comes from a wide variety of

motives, not all of them completely pure. It is easier for an
Englishman to send money to the United States than to face
the problems of his own slums; it even helps him achieve
the kind of superiority an American white racist gets
when he contributes to a missionary fund for Africans. And
the Interchurch Aid director of one Scandinavian country
confided that his committee was sending money to the
Delta Ministry "to call attention to America's untenable
position in Vietnam."

The overriding motive, of course, was Christian concern
and, in many cases, a recognition that the problems of the
Delta are common to all the world today.

The Delta Ministry's experiences have involved not just
civil rights, and not just southern injustice. The battle of
the poor of Mississippi, in which DM joined, is part of a
world-wide battle for social, economic, and political justice.
The more I lived in Mississippi, the more I was aware that
conditions there differed from conditions in the North—or
in Africa, Asia, and Europe—only in sophistication and sub-
tlety. I saw the truth of Robert Parris Moses' reminder:
"Mississippi should not be a moral lightning rod, drawing
our anger, but a mirror in which the rest of the nation sees
itself."

The black people of Mississippi, though many of them
could not express it in scholarly terms, were aware that
their struggle was a world-wide one. Their instinctive sympathy for the Vietnamese and their antipathy to the war
is one sign of this; their pride in the achievements of the
emerging African peoples is another. (In Winstonville,
there is a youngster whose middle name is Kenyatta.)

The white segregationists are aware of the nature of the
struggle we're in, too. In February 1968, Senator Eastland
made political hay back home by introducing a congressional resolution urging the United States government to

send military aid to South Africa. A week earlier, the Consul General of South Africa received a standing ovation from a combined meeting of the civic luncheon clubs of Cleveland, Mississippi, after a speech there.

When I went to England in June 1966 to speak about the Delta Ministry to a world Interchurch Aid conference, I ran into signs of this world struggle right away. The taxi driver on the way in from the London airport saw two black men on the street and volunteered, "Bloody blacks are takin' over this town, you know." The *London Times* had a front-page picture of the tear-gassing, in Canton, Mississippi, of the Meredith Marchers the night before; I had left Canton and the march that night. At speakers' corner in Hyde Park, eight of the ten men on soapboxes were speaking about some aspects of racial injustice.

While in London, I tried to contact the owners of Delta and Pine Lands Plantation, the largest (38,000 acres) in the Delta. The plantation has been owned for fifty years by Fine Spinners and Doublers, Ltd., which owns forty other companies; Fine Spinners in turn is owned by Courtauld's a huge industrial firm. I was unsuccessful in reaching anybody in authority to ask if they knew of the conditions on the plantation, which are much like those of any other Delta farm.

At the Interchurch Aid meeting, I heard churchmen from many lands talk of absentee landlords, of peonage and serfdom, of hardened class lines, of political exclusion, of the widening gap between the affluent and the poor, about the increasing centralization of the world's economic power, and the resulting preservation of the status quo.

Two things stuck out like an accusing finger: (1) the "have-nots" are mostly dark-skinned, and the "haves" are light-skinned; (2) the established Church identifiies itself largely with the "haves."

The Delta was very much in my mind as I heard Professor S. L. Parmar of India analyze the world Church's role in the struggle of developing countries:

First, he said, "Our involvement has been partial. After an initial 'revolutionary' step we have tended to support order rather than justice. The Church created a new awareness of community and then tended to become a closed community, living for itself." It grew, he said, "because of self-denial, but gradually made more and more compromises, for self-preservation. As such it has failed to recognize its own offspring in some of the revolutionary ferment which characterizes developing nations."

Second, he said, the relationships between the giving churches in the richer nations and the receiving churches in poorer lands had led to a distortion of the idea of partnership. "Lack of stewardship, withdrawal from involvement in social processes, self-interest, and paternalistic patterns of assistance exemplify this."

Third, the Church in a developing nation sometimes develops a "defeatist minority complex," which is a "strange contradiction to the history and heritage of the Church." Such a Church rationalizes its lack of involvement by coming to believe in a self-preservative "Church vs. World" theology, and withdraws into a protective "spiritualistic" shell.

And fourth, he pointed out that sometimes "the social and economic action of the Church is intended to dampen and weaken revolutionary forces rather than inject idealism and purpose in the revolution."

As an organization receiving Interchurch Aid, DM is a living symbol, to American and overseas churchman alike, of the new relationship between United States churches and the rest of the world. No more is it a mother-daughter relationship.

As a "foreign mission" in America, DM made many white southerners puzzled and angry, and thus began an educational process in which they had to *think* about the role of the Church in society.

It has managed to remain open to the needs and desires of the people to whom it is a servant. Its presence reminds black people in the Delta that people all around the world are on their side in the struggle.

And amidst continual hostility from preachers and deacons, DM is one reminder that in many places the Church, like its founder, still identifies with the poor and the voiceless.

# 13. White Power

"*Am I not safe in saying that Southern Senators and Congressmen are pretty well in control? In the House of Representatives there are 13 Southerners holding committee chairmanships among the 20 standing committees. In the Senate there are 10 out of 16.*

"*Committees are the places where the power is exercised, isn't it?*"
   —*Senator John Sparkman*, radio interview, quoted in
   THE NEW YORK TIMES MAGAZINE,
      November 7, 1965

"*Mississippi is a white man's country, and by the eternal God, we'll run it.*" —YAZOO CITY BANNER
      July 31, 1875

THE YEAR 1966 WAS a busy one for the Mississippi legislature.

That was the year in which it became obvious that the state's black citizens were taking seriously the Voting Rights Act, passed in June 1965. Before the law was passed, there were 28,500 black voters registered in the state: about 6.7 percent of the eligible residents. By the fall of 1967, there were 170,000 registered, and a year later, 263,000.

It was obvious to many of the legislators that the status

quo was in danger. Many counties had black majorities; even in counties which were predominantly white, one or two beats might have a black majority. And who could forget that the Delta, which had always fought to maintain its unity as the First Congressional District, was two-thirds black?

Within a matter of weeks the Mississippi legislature took these steps:

1. Passed a bill allowing counties to choose their five supervisors at large, rather than from each beat.

2. Submitted to the voters a constitutional amendment empowering the legislature, by a two-thirds vote, to merge any two counties.

3. Divided the Delta congressional district into three pieces and combined each piece with a block of counties which was overwhelmingly white in population.

4. Set up the machinery to make the office of county superintendent of schools appointive, instead of elective.

5. Passed a law disqualifying anyone who votes in the June primary from running as an independent in the fall general election. (This one took 19 Negro candidates out of the running at one swipe.)

6. Raised qualifying fees and the number of certified signatures needed to become a candidate—in some cases, by tenfold.

7. Passed a law (when it looked as though black candidates in several counties might run a good race for school trustee) moving the date for qualification to forty-eight hours after the law was passed—and stiffening the requirements for qualification.

Actually, the process was nothing new for either black man or white in Mississippi. For a century, whites in power have been using legal means—and some illegal—to keep blacks out of power.

Before the Voting Rights Act it had been the long eighteen-question registration form and the absolute decision power of the registrar which kept black citizens from voting and running for office in some counties. In other counties, it was fear. In some, it was the three long trips to the county courthouse: to pay the last year's poll tax, to pay this year's tax, and then to register. For plantation workers in some counties, it could be a forty-mile round trip each time.

So these tactics were not new to the whites who devised them nor to the blacks who suffered under them. In fact, they were only a small part of a whole system of power.

Rufus Hurns of Glen Allan filed an affidavit after one of the annual Department of Agriculture ASCS (crop allotment) committee elections. He shows what it's like to be on the wrong end of the system:

> The sheriff came to me on this morning. He asked me if I knew the civil rights workers had my name on the ASCS petition to run for community committee and that I would be running against his brother.
>
> I told him the people had asked me to run and I told them I would. Therefore I knew my name was there.
>
> I asked the sheriff would it be any danger or harm my name being there. He said certainly it wouldn't be any value or profit and he advised me as a friend to go to the county agent and take my name off. He said he just wanted to protect his neighbors.
>
> I presumed from his conversation it was quite a risk. I thanked him and went down to the ASCS office and told the lady in the office to take my name off.

The ASCS committee decides how much cotton each farmer can raise each year out of the strictly limited allotment assigned the county. The committees, although this is a federal program, have always been all white.

White power is the Edwards, Mississippi, city council selling the town swimming pool to the garden club for a dollar, to keep it segregated.

White power is the county Farmers Home Administration committee (made up of white planters) delaying the loan of a black farmer because he's running for county supervisor.

White power is refusing federal surplus commodities to plantation workers unless they have a paper from the boss man saying they deserve it.

And white power, if you have enough of it, is thumbing your nose at the Voting Rights Act, as detailed in this excerpt from a column by Drew Pearson:

> A delegation of 12 Democratic congressmen called on Attorney General Nick Katzenbach the other day to urge him to appoint more reg'strars to record Negro voters in Mississippi, especially in Sunflower county, home of Sen. "Big Jim" Eastland.
>
> The meeting was off the record. However, this column can report that the 12 got absolutely nowhere. The attorney general politely but flatly refused to put registrars in the home county of the senator who rules over the Senate Judiciary Committee, and passes on Justice Department business.

Senator Eastland's influence with the Justice Department is a symbol of two things every northerner ought to keep in mind when he is discussing Mississippi and white power: First, the politicians of Mississippi wield power in the federal government in a way that affects every American citizen. Second, the Mississippi system continues because of the apathy, tacit consent, or active support of the rest of the country.

Eastland, a Delta plantation owner, was identified by *The New York Times* as the "key figure in the revolt against confirmation" of Supreme Court Justice Abe Fortas as Chief Justice—an action that affects every citizen. But

Eastland might not be senator at all if the rest of the nation had insisted on strict enforcement of federal law over the last twenty years.

Take a look at some of the Mississippi politicians who influence your life.

Senator John Stennis is the second-ranking member, and heir apparent to Richard Russell as chairman, of the Senate Armed Forces Committee. He is chairman of the Preparedness Subcommittee, a member of the Appropriations Committee, and chairman of the new "watchdog" committee on Standards and Conduct. He has a lot to say about how many soldiers go to Vietnam, and has fought like a bulldog, with considerable success, to kill CDGM's Head Start program from the day it was first instituted. He usually sits in for Russell on the Defense Appropriations Subcommittee, which concerns itself with around two-thirds of the whole federal budget.

Senator James O. Eastland owns 5800 acres of rich Delta cotton land, but he spends his time cultivating the Senate. He is chairman of the Judiciary Committee, which examines and passes on every appointment to a federal judgeship. He once held up the appointment of a New York federal judge for more than a year because of her involvement in civil rights cases.

Eastland persuaded John F. Kennedy to make an outspoken segregationist, Harold Cox, his first appointment to the federal bench; apparently it was the prerequisite for Judiciary Committee approval of the rest of the judges Kennedy wanted to name. Eastland is also chairman of the Senate Internal Security Subcommittee (the upper chamber's version of the House Unamerican Activities Committee), which is empowered to hunt subversives coast to coast.

And the conservative nature of the FBI and its recognized reluctance to involve itself in civil rights matters (except to investigate "communist influence") is not the result alone of J. Edgar Hoover's leadership; the Judiciary Committee influence on program and budget is strong there, too.

Representative William Colmer of Mississippi is chairman of the House Rules Committee, which must clear all new legislation. He is fourth in seniority in the whole House, and as Rules chairman he was the key man stopping a strong gun-control law.

Representative Thomas Abernethy ranks high on the Agriculture Committee and is number-two man on the District of Columbia Committee—the southern-dominated committee which has ruled the District like a plantation.

All these men, because of the seniority system (and the disfranchisement of black voters, which gave them the seniority), have the power to affect the whole country. But the most influential of Mississippi's congressmen may be the least known: Congressman Jamie Whitten of the Delta.

There is no farmer in the country whose life has not been directly affected by the wishes and whims of Jamie Whitten, and there are few consumers of farm produce who are not also affected. He is chairman of the Subcommittee on Agricultural Appropriations—with the power over the budget of the Agriculture Department.

"We don't even spit," an Agriculture Department official once admitted to me, "unless Whitten first clears his throat." Among the issues in which Whitten has taken a personal interest are subsidies, price supports, farm labor conditions and wages, crop allotments, and the distribution of surplus commodities.

When an embarrassed and angry Secretary Orville Freeman tried to defend his actions in turning back to the Treasury more than two million dollars in unused appropriations for feeding the hungry, he was defending a policy which most observers believe was set for him by Congressman

Whitten. The Delta Ministry was in a continual struggle for four years to get the Agriculture Department to come up with a fair and useful program of assistance to hungry people; the name of Whitten always came up in off-the-record discussions.

That's one side of the coin: the power Mississippi congressmen have over all of us. The other side is the responsibility we all have for the way Mississippi is.

The Freedom Democratic Patry appealed to your congressman, along with all the rest, to obey the law in respect to the election of the five Mississippi congressmen in the fall of 1964. Approximately one-fourth of the Congress voted in favor of the FDP challenge, on the legal grounds that the exclusion of Negroes from voting made the 1964 Mississippi congressional election unlawful. The other three-fourths of the Congress did not feel enough pressure from constituents to go along.

And if that doesn't appeal to your sense of "law and order," what about this: Mississippi was re-admitted to the Union after the Civil War on the condition that discrimination be outlawed—and with the express guarantee that if ever again the state discriminated against its black citizens, it would be occupied by troops and once again made a ward of the federal government. That didn't happen, of course, even when the number of registered Negro voters dropped in ten years from 260,000 to 8,000 just before the turn of the century.

The nation's business is part of Mississippi business, too. Most of the large factories in Mississippi are branches of national firms—but until 1967 most insisted they had to "conform to local custom." This is a euphemism for discrimination in hiring. The nationally owned plants, which because of their outside base might have set an example and helped break the barrier, were indistinguishable from the plants owned by the local White Citizens Council leaders.

What's more, many of these "outside" plants had come for the express purpose of taking advantage of cheap, unorganized labor. Most had the unwritten guarantee of the local authorities that they would not be troubled by unions. Thus many citizens, white as well as black, found themselves trapped in a low-wage system with their own town government allied with the plant management against them.

The willingness of northern firms to "conform" even in the most flagrant abuses was demonstrated in December 1967 when twenty-two successful black candidates found that northern insurance companies wouldn't bond them. The bond was necessary to take office; otherwise the positions would, under law, be declared vacant. All the white candidates were bonded, but it took six weeks of pressure and publicity from lawyers, civil rights groups, and the National Council of Churches to get the insurance companies to write bond on those black citizens. (The companies claimed the refusal had been strictly for business reasons, but Charles Evers pointed out: "A lot of poor whites don't even own a chicken, and they get bonded.")

This willingness of business to stick with the status quo is paralleled by much of the activity of the federal government. It is true that much of the change in Mississippi in the last few years has come because of federal pressure, and the dogged perseverance of Justice Department agents. But for every federal man working for change, there has been one supporting "the way things are."

While Justice Department men were overseeing registration in Mississippi one fall, for example, we were visited by the two county agents of Washington County. They came into the Greenville office, the white one walking ahead of the black one, and asked to see the person in charge. I pointed out Mrs. Barnes' office, and the white agent went down the hall to knock on her door.

But as soon as he saw that Mrs. Barnes was black, he came back and took a seat by the front door. His black partner got up without a word and went back to Mrs. Barnes' office to state their business. It was typical, segregated, Department of Agriculture procedure.

The Agriculture Department's sensitivity to human need was demonstrated in a meeting one hot night in a crowded frame church in Tutwiler, in Tallahatchie County. Solomon Gort, DM's county director there, had called the meeting, because Agriculture was pushing a change from surplus commodities to the food stamp plan, and an Agriculture representative had expressed doubt that there was anyone in the county who couldn't afford the two dollars per months per each member of the family to buy the stamps.

That night sixty-seven people signed a petition, in front of the USDA man's eyes, stating that they had had no cash income for the past two months, and didn't foresee any during the next year. A dozen people told their stories in the meeting, as the Agriculture man fidgeted.

Then he stood up to reply. "I have a newspaper clipping here," he said, "which means a lot to me. It gives a quotation from Abraham Lincoln, in which he says that the only things we really appreciate are the things we help do ourselves.

"Now," he said, "if we just give you commodities, it isn't going to be good for your self-respect. The stamp program gives you a chance to participate."

A bent, white-haired lady stood up. "Mister," she said, "Don't you understand? We got nothin' to participate with. My boss man, I cooked and chopped cotton for for thirty-two years, says he can't use me this year, and not any more at all."

Agriculture rose again, with a sorrowful smile. "I sympathize with your problem." he said, "but it still is not good for people to be dependent." He turned to Gort. "I have another clipping here; shall I read it?"

'Go ahead, baby," said the Reverend Mr. Gort. "It's your neck." The man from Agriculture sat down.

And the Justice Department, for all its promises, sent federal registrars to only fifty-eight counties in the whole deep South. Fewer than half of Mississippi's eighty-two counties got the boost that came from having a registrar come in. And for a long time the Justice men refused to set up mobile registration trailers, going out to the fields to sign people up, even though it was obvious that the long trip to a single registration center and the limitations of a long working day made signing up impossible for most plantation workers. The burden for registration has been, by and large, on the civil rights organizations; the federal government removed some of the hurdles, but left the logistics to private groups.

The FBI and the Justice Department have been slow to investigate police who used their powers to deny citizens their rights. The Reverend Clint Collier, an FDP candidate for Congress in 1966, was continually and openly harassed by Neshoba County's famous law enforcement organization. He was beaten several times by white men. But no action was ever taken by the government.

Nor was there any action when the FDP pointed out that of ninety-three polling places in Hinds County (which includes Jackson), not one was in a Negro neighborhood.

The FBI delayed for hours doing anything about the frantic calls from friends of Goodman, Chaney, and Schwerner. Had the federal men shown interest and called the sheriff's office when they themselves were first notified, the three young men might not have died. They were still alive and in jail when the FBI was first called.

It is true, as Dr. King once pointed out, that many federal men in the South are themselves native southerners. And their selection and training, at least in the FBI, tends to make them more conservative. Add to this fact that most FBI men rely upon a close working relationship with the local police, and you see why most civil rights workers have little respect, and even less trust, for J. Edgar Hoover's representatives. There are exceptions, of course, and the word quickly gets around that "there is one guy you can trust."

The federal courts in Mississippi, thanks in large part to the influence of Eastland on appointments, are not much help either. Judges Dan Russell and Harold Cox have publicly stated their opposition to desegregation; Judge Coleman is a former governor of Mississippi. The three of them as a panel have upheld each of the first five laws in the list at the beginning of this chapter.

Judge Cox presided over various court appearances of the men accused of killing Goodman, Chaney, and Schwerner. Several times he postponed the trials indefinitely, on his own initiative. Once, two and a half years after the murders, he postponed the trial because he was angry over reports about the Child Development Group of Mississippi; he told the Justice Department he wouldn't reconvene the trial until it began an investigation of the Head Start program.

Because of the delays and the relatively low bail of $10,000 set by Cox, Sam H. Bowers was still walking around free four years after the Neshoba County murders. More important, he was free in January 1966 when the FBI charges he planned and ordered the death of Vernon Dahmer.

He was convicted October 20, 1967, of a federal charge in connection with the Neshoba County killings, but continued free on appeal bond and presided at meetings of the

White Knights of the Ku Klux Klan, which he heads. He was tried on an arson charge in connection with Dahmer's death, but went free after a deadlock jury—eleven to one for conviction—resulted in a mistrial.

With this kind of history in the federal courts, it's no wonder black men and women see a credibility gap when they're urged to "work sensibly, through the courts."

Many Mississippians would like to believe—and have the rest of the nation believe—that the system of discrimination is maintained by a small minority of extremists, nuts, and crackpots. But there are two things wrong with such a belief:

First, the system which keeps the black man in "his place" depends upon many prominent, powerful, and well-educated persons for its continuation: newspaper publishers, political leaders, plantation owners, and industrialists. They are not rednecks or crackers; Stennis is a Phi Beta Kappa and even Sam H. Bowers had two years of college and is a successful businessman. Most of the men are not haters; they are family men, church men, who are so caught up in a social and economic system that they are blinded to what it is doing to them and to the men they exploit.

Second, those who oppose the system of oppression and deprivation, if they exist in any significant number, apparently dare not speak out. Until late in 1967, you could count on your fingers the white leaders of Mississippi who have unequivocally called for changes which would make black men first-class citizens. They were well aware of the example of the Reverend Donald Thompson, the Unitarian minister critically wounded by a shotgun blast from a passing car in Jackson, or of Hazel Brannon Smith, nearly bankrupted and often physically threatened because of her editorial courage.

The most outspoken white Mississippians for a long time could hardly go beyond calls for "law and order" (this was in the days when "violence" brought to mind visions of the Ku Klux Klan, not rioters). Even the most "respectable" civil rights activities—voter drives, Head Start, or relief for the poor—failed to bring support.

The sad fact is that the so-called "moderate" leadership in a town bears responsibility for the climate which permits —or prevents—the actions of an extremist. When we moved to Greenville, we were told that the city fathers would allow no violence to mar the image of their fair city. For our safety, a police car sat across the street all the time the mover was unloading our furniture. When a Negro child was assaulted on Nelson Street one night, the police came to the DM for help and quickly tracked down his white assailant. During the two years we lived in Greenville, there were no bombings or other acts of overt racial violence.

By contrast, McComb had nineteen bombings in less than a month. And, significantly, the bombings stopped the day the first contingent of Presbyterian preachers arrived in town, bringing publicity and northern concern with them. When the power structure—the "moderate" leaders of the town, the bankers and businessmen—put out the word that bombings would no longer be tolerated, they stopped.

In *Mississippi: The Closed Society* (New York, 1966), James Silver quotes an Episcopal clergyman who was run out of the state by the extremists: "The great disappointment was that persons of prominence who would give you to understand they never paid dues to the Citizens Council gave all the support the Citizens Council could hope for by their silence."

The Delta Ministry was always in hot water with the moderates, of course. The moderate view says, in effect, that you must work through the existing power structure to improve the lot of the poor, because the power structure has such firm control that this is the only way.

But when you work only through the power structure, you become involved in a series of compromises; you must bargain and make trades. Soon you find that because the structure itself has corruption, you are becoming corrupted.

The radicals argue that the idea of a small change here and a small change there, each change accompanied by a minor readjustment or weakening of goals, just is not going to do the job; a rebuilding of the entire society is what is needed. Most of the Delta Ministry staff subscribed to this view.

Many times we were urged, "Don't rock the boat. Don't cut off communication. You'll hurt your own cause. You'll make it impossible for us, the moderates, to bring about the changes we'd like to make."

It boiled down to a plea by men who, no matter how well intentioned they thought they were or how ably they had rationalized their attitudes, still were thinking first of their own skins.

They were also prisoners of the instinctive presumption that there is always a middle way. But there are times and instances when there is not a middle way—when there is a right side and a wrong side. There are times when compromise produces such a weakening of the situation that it is not worth the struggle any more—and thus, times when compromise itself is wrong.

This is not to say that the Delta Ministry was somehow infallibly on the right side each time. Taking a firm stand doesn't guarantee that it is the right one. But the men whose souls are bound to shrivel, it seems to me, are those who shrink from taking the stand, sticking out the neck, making a move, correcting a falsehood, standing with someone who is already halfway out on the plank.

During one of his thirty sojourns in jail, Martin Luther King wrote:

I have almost reached the regrettable conclusion that the Negro's great stumbling block in his stride toward freedom is not the White Citizen's Counciler or the Ku Klux Klanner but the white moderate who is more devoted to "order" than to justice; who prefers a negative peace which is the absence of tension to a positive peace which is the presence of justice; who constantly says, "I agree with you in the goal you seek, but I cannot agree with your methods;" who paternalistically believes he can set the timetable for another man's freedom . . . and who constantly advises the Negro to wait for "a more convenient season."

The inability of the Mississippi white leadership to work in even the most "respectable" kind of program—if that program means shifting power into new hands—is demonstrated in the story of the Delta Opportunity Corporation. Today it is a successful and noncontroversial program which has been featured in *Fortune* magazine and partially sponsored by the Southern Presbyterian church; when it began, though, it was under attack by the newspapers, the clergy, the police, a mayor, the governor, several congressmen, and both United States senators from Mississippi.

The idea for the Delta Opportunities Corporation originally came from a speech made on the House floor by Congressman Henry Reuss, a Democrat from Wisconsin. The Congressman had been to Mississippi and had seen some of its problems; his son Mike had been a civil rights volunteer in West Point early in 1965 and had been arrested twice.

Not long after returning from a trip to help his son, Congressman Reuss made a speech that said, in effect, let's get off Mississippi's back and give her a hand. He explained that the state's problems are mostly economic, and pointed out how certain economic development bills recently passed or still under consideration would help ease those problems.

Sometime that summer Reuss talked with Art Thomas. He proposed that the Delta Ministry try to bring together a group of native Mississippians from nine or ten counties in the southern half of the Delta and help them set up a nonprofit corporation. Such a corporation could receive and administer federal funds in such fields as job training, economic development, low-cost housing, and small business opportunities.

With the new rent-supplement bill, he pointed out, you could build decent cooperative housing for people making as little as $1,000 a year. You could get money to train Negro store owners, many of whom were victimized regularly by white wholesalers, in bookkeeping, inventory control, and advertising.

After some intense recruiting by friends in ten counties, a fifty-man committee came together. There were only two or three college graduates on the whole committee. The rest were people whose only credentials were a record of successful leadership in their own communities. Nineteen were farmers; there were mail carriers, housewives, a druggist, a cook. There were only two ministers in the lot.

There was excitement in the smoky air of the Greenville office that day. I think nearly everybody there actually believed that it would work—that the United States government was actually going to allow Mississippi Negroes to put together and administer programs of their own choosing, rather than programs selected and run on their behalf by moderate whites and "responsible" Negroes.

After discussing it all day long, the committee agreed to apply for a charter for "Delta Opportunities Corporation" and to start with three relatively small projects:

They would ask the Department of Commerce to help in a study of the economic problems of the ten counties involved, so the area could be officially designated as a redevelopment area. This would make the south Delta eligible for grants and loans for water and sewage systems, industrial parks, health facilities, tourist parks, streets, bridges, reservoirs, and vocational schools—and make federal loans to private, job-creating industries much easier to get.

They would apply under the new 221(d)3 housing act for 100 percent financing for low-cost housing projects and seek rental supplements for those who qualified: the elderly, the handicapped, and those presently occupying substandard housing.

And they would work with the Small Business Administration to get training and loans for men who wanted to expand their operations but had always been hampered by ignorance and the inability to get sufficient cash from white-controlled banks.

At the committee's request, we went through all the motions of informing the "proper" people of our plans. We wrote the Mississippi Economic Council, the Greenville Chamber of Commerce and Greenville's Mayor Pat Dunne. Seeking white members for the board, we talked to more than a dozen white moderates who were reasonably trustworthy and even—in desperation—to a few who were obviously not. Only one man agreed to let his name be used, and he later withdrew. (One woman, known widely for her liberal activities, delayed an answer until she had talked to her husband. Then it was "no." "He owns a store," she said, "and he'd like to stay in business. He has Klan customers, and no matter how respectable this program is, they aren't going to like my working with the Delta Ministry.")

We ran into more discouragement in Washington. The steering committee of Delta Opportunities Corporation sent two of its members—Thelma Barnes and Clarence Hall—with Al Winham and me to the capital on September 9 to get specific information on the proposed projects.

Thanks to Congressman Reuss and some of his colleagues,

Thelma Barnes and friend at Freedom City (*Dan Guravich*)

we found a warm welcome in many offices. Fourteen congressmen agreed to have their pictures taken with us, as a gesture of support. We were assured of good wishes by civil servants and appointed officials in the Department of Commerce, the Office of Economic Opportunity, the Department of Housing and Urban Development, the Department of Agriculture, and the Small Business Administration.

And that's all we brought back with us: warm good wishes.

The Small Business Administration, we were told, was broke; they had spent all available loan money on the victims of Hurricane Betsy in New Orleans. The Department óf Commerce people told us we needed somebody with experience; if we could get a man with proven success in a large-scale business to take personal charge of our enterprise, they could arrange huge loans for a new factory. When Clarence Hall explained the difficulty of getting a man with big-business experience in an area where the whole system kept anybody from getting such experience, the Commerce people were sympathetic but, they said, helpless.

Several of the people we conferred with questioned us at length about the "qualifications" of the board members. Their questions were so similar that it was obvious somebody had been spreading the word. But their questions also reflected the vague fears all of us who are "educated" and relatively secure have of the mass of the people. Though we don't admit it, most of us don't really think the poor are capable of a voice in government.

The Delta Opportunities members were leaders in the truest sense; they had been selected from their own communities by people who trusted and respected their judgment. Many of them were landowners, all had good credit, none had been convicted of a crime (except a civil rights arrest or two). But they didn't have *names*. They hadn't allied themselves with whites who could vouch for them as "responsible," who could put them up for various meaningless posts on boards which needed a black face or two. Theirs was real leadership, conferred by the people rather than by the powerful, but it wasn't the kind which the government was used to dealing with.

"Why don't you get ——— on your board," an official would say. "He's well known up here."

"He doesn't have the respect of the people in his county any more," someone would say. But it was like talking to a brick wall.

There were two Washington officials who didn't even bother to talk to us. They were our Mississippi congressmen, John Bell Williams and Jamie Whitten. Both had given us appointments, but upon our arrival at each office we found that the men had suddenly been called away.

In several other offices we found people concerned and friendly, but limited by regulations which required a down payment, or a credit rating, or a steady income. We soon concluded that the poverty program had little to offer a person making less than $1500 a year, and we were trying to get help for people whose median income was less than a third of that.

We came away from the Washington trip let down, but not without hope. We knew we had the unshakable backing of Congressman Reuss; *he* believed the poor were capable of assuming responsibility, and as a Democrat with growing seniority, he was in a position to help us. He knew we were unpopular, but he was one Washingtonian who wasn't afraid to get involved with us.

The opposition didn't really get organized until around the end of September. Then one day I got a call from Reuss's office; Aaron Henry and Andy Carr of Coahoma County had called on the congressman that morning. We knew Henry; once a leader of COFO and FDP candidate for governor in the Freedom Vote, he had been increasingly isolated from the growing movement since the FDP challenge at the 1964 Democratic convention when he had voted to accept the compromise seating plan. Carr, we soon found out, was a moderate white plantation owner with powerful connections in Washington.

Carr, Reuss's office told us, had come to Washington with the apparent purpose of discrediting the Delta Ministry in the Congressman's eyes. Using DM's involvement in the CDGM Head Start, which was then under loud and heavy attack from Senator Stennis, Carr had tried to convince Reuss that entrusting government money to so irresponsible an outfit was dangerous.

Aaron Henry, a member of the Delta Opportunities board and a member of the Delta Ministry commission, did not add to the charges. He merely sat silently by, we were told, while Carr talked.

The Congressman, of course, could see through this approach. But he urged us to begin trying harder for just a few white people and "name" Negroes to pad out the board of directors; this apparently was fast becoming a political necessity, and could be done, he said, as long as it didn't endanger the control held by the real local leaders.

The power of a name was brought home to us immediately, in fact. Carr and Henry had made other visits in Washington. And within a few days it was announced that Coahoma Opportunities, Inc., had been formed—a nonprofit corporation to receive federal funds in Coahoma County. Andy Carr and Aaron Henry were among the top officers. And promises of several hundred thousand dollars in preliminary funds had already been made.

It was to be eighteen months before our new baby, Delta Opportunities, got one cent.

Another indication that somebody in Washington was watching came on September 30. Robert Allen and Paul Scott, syndicated columnists, singled out Delta Opportunities as a prime example of "grass-roots propaganda and politics-loaded activities funded by anti-poverty money." Somebody had fed them the information that, "in effect, DOC aims to make itself a kind of Tammany Hall doing favors (collecting and distributing federal grants) for its largely Negro constituents." Stronger on innuendo than on information, the pair called DOC "an outgrowth of a $1.4 million Head Start project for pre-school children in Mississippi," and "masterminded" by the same group that conducted CDGM.

The next morning, October 19, I got a call from the United Press International "stringer" correspondent in Greenville.

"Why did —— leave the staff?" he wanted to know. I told him the reason: fatigue and poor health, resulting from a year of unrelenting pressure.

"But we have a photostat of a police record and a doctor's report here, which show that he's a convicted homosexual. Seems to me it would be a lot better for Delta Ministry if you admit that he was discharged because of his being a homo. If it gets released from here, you're going to catch a lot of heat."

The man had always been friendly, and I told him the truth: "As far as I know, it's a lie. I do know that it had nothing to do with his leaving Delta Ministry."

As soon as he hung up, I told Art Thomas, and we put in a long-distance call to the former staffer. "These rumors have been around a long time," Art told me as he dialed. "The chief of police helped spread them. There's nothing to them, but we'd better be sure."

When the call went through, Art told him what was happening. "For God's sake, if there's anything to it, tell us so we can have our ammunition ready."

No, the voice on the other end said, there's nothing to it. No police record and no doctor's report. The reporter was obviously fishing for information.

I didn't bother to call the UPI man back. No story ever appeared, of course. And I never got around to filing a complaint with the news service about the violation of journalistic ethics. Within a few months the man resigned to become public relations man for Senator Eastland.

Meanwhile, Clarence Hall had been fired. He had worked four years at a northern-owned factory in Greenville, since the farm was too small to support his family alone. Despite a good record there, he was dismissed—for being absent the four days he had spent in Washington for DOC.

This may have been one of the best things to come out of the vendetta against Delta Opportunities, however. Mr. Hall was now available to join the Delta Ministry staff; he became Issaquena County project director, Freedom City farming director, and a welcome step in the shift in DM personnel from "outsiders" to native Mississippians.

At just about the same time, Mayor Pat Dunne of Greenville was calling a meeting. He called in the "responsible Negro leaders" of the town and urged them to sign a statement requesting that the Delta Ministry leave Mississippi. Although several of the men there had had serious differences with DM—usually the predictable differences related to personalities—they refused to sign.

The *Delta Democrat-Times* had carried an editorial of halfhearted approval for the Delta Opportunities idea, after Art had called upon the elder Hodding Carter and explained the program. The editorial is worth reading, because it shows the limited distance the most "liberal" editor in the most "liberal" town in Mississippi was able to stick out his neck for so reasonable a program:

### A Vacuum And Delta Ministry

Of the controversial Delta Ministry, a number of whose activities and some of whose personnel we have opposed, one thing can be said with certainty. At the time of its establishment it filled a vacuum which was largely created by the white community itself. A considerable part of our local white and Negro leadership has tried in the past year to fill that vacuum. This is as it should be.

It is too early to try to pass judgment upon the Delta Ministry's plan to sponsor actively a number of economic projects, using federal funds, for the material benefit of a ten-county Delta area. *But we cannot see any reason, at first glance, to oppose the program as outlined* if it does not collide with nor duplicate local or county projects which will also need money from the government [italics added].

But this area needs all the responsible help it can get in respect to economic development. We desperately need urban renewal programs and encouragement for small business. Our slums need to be replaced with decent, low cost housing. Somebody has to carry the ball.

Our civic leaders and elected officials can carry the ball if they want to. In such case the proposed undertaking of the Delta Ministry may well be secondary if indeed it will be needed at all. But as of now we should not turn down any serious proposals for the physical and social improvement of our area. This vacuum still exists.

Mrs. Carter, who because of her husband's serious eye troubles carried major responsibility for editing the paper that year, explained to me later in the week: "I see a newspaper as a ship, carrying valuable learning and leadership for the community. If, however, the ship deliberately makes itself a target and causes so much commotion that it gets sunk by the enemy, then it no longer can carry its important cargo.

"Thus if it seems that we are playing it safe, it is in order to keep the paper alive so we can continue to provide leadership."

A week later the paper ran an editorial that, in effect, repudiated the other one. "The Vacuum Still Exists," the headline read, and the article ran three and a half times as long as the favorable one.

The two most serious blows, of all the events apparently tied to the birth of Delta Opportunities, were still to come.

With the help of the Foundation for Cooperative Housing, a private agency with wide experience in building with government money, the DOC planned to build ten thousand homes in the Delta. These would be owned cooperatively by the tenants, not rented; the idea of owning one's home had special attraction for people whose life on plantations had been symbolized by dependence and impermanence.

To build the units at a price that would make them available to people earning as little as $1,000 a year, DOC had to count on occupancy by a certain percentage of people who would be getting rent supplements. But the rent-supplement program was having rough going in Congress; it drew fire from most conservative congressmen and apparently from several active lobbyists. Eventually it squeaked through both houses, but the House bill failed to provide any money to run the program. The question of funding was left to a Senate-House conference committee, which failed to put the money back in.

We had a promising program and no money available to run it for more than a year. The disappointment was made more bitter when congressional staffers told us that Congressman Jamie Whitten of the Delta had been on the conference committee, that he had strongly fought against the funding, and that his opposition was openly based, among other things, on his fears that Delta Opportunities might succeed.

And finally, the builder backed out. One of the biggest and most secure in the state, a moderate who had always dealt politely with DM, he had originally agreed to erect the ten thousand housing units. One thousand of the homes were to be on land just outside the Greenville city limits, and in construction alone represented eight million dollars to the Greenville economy.

But he called Mrs. Barnes, and said he wanted out. At first he was vague about his reasons. He had "changed his mind." He was "too busy this year."

Finally Mrs. Barnes went over to the man's office, and demanded to know why he was giving up on an eight-million-dollar job.

"As a matter of fact," he said, "local leaders called me in, and they've all agreed that there is going to be trouble on this project with zoning, with water, with sewers, with right-of-way, with fire protection, with building permits—with every step you make. And that's going to be true as long as the Delta Ministry has anything to do with it."

The housing project is probably dead. Mayor Dunne,

working with "safer" groups, has been promising to get funds for housing—though it will undoubtedly be publicly owned rental property.

Delta Opportunities had many more disappointments. Al Winham of our staff worked for more than a year trying to untangle the political snarls and then got caught in the 1967 budget cut, fired with two weeks' notice.

It took thousands of dollars in time and travel. It took the air base incident and more patience than most people had. But finally DOC got funded, in spring 1967. The program was to provide fifty dispossessed plantation families with thirty hours a week of training in literacy and basic adult education, plus a weekly subsistence payment for eleven months. And it would provide materials and training so the families could construct, under supervision, their own homes at Freedom City.

The money for the materials came from one of America's biggest philanthropic foundations. Even this was held up for three months after the government money came through, because the foundation was hesitant about trusting "unknown" poor people with hard cash; it finally insisted on giving the money to the National Council of Churches to administer and transmit to DOC.

The "system" we encountered in all this was not a neatly organized affair that could be diagrammed on a chart. It is not the kind of thing in which conscious policy decisions are made by a board of directors.

Instead, it appears that the itch for conformity, the yen for job security among government employees, the greed of men in power have much to do with holding the system together. By its very nature—and not necessarily by any consciously directed antipathy—the system discriminates against the poor, the nameless, the powerless, the dark-skinned, the "radicals," the boat rockers.

# 14. The New Mississippi

"By and large, the African slaves brought to America were those who otherwise would have been killed, and often eaten.

"So the growth of the slave trade made it possible for captive Negroes to survive and beget children."

—JACKSON CLARION-LEDGER

EXCEPT FOR THE ONE BIG THING, Joseph Williams would have been a natural candidate for the board of supervisors of Yazoo County. Like most other aspirants for office in Mississippi, he's a deacon and Sunday school teacher in a Baptist church, a World War II veteran with five battle stars, and a successful farmer. Unlike many of the candidates, he's a good speaker, with a warm, resonant voice and a sense of humor.

But since he's black, some white farmers in his area held a meeting the week after he announced his candidacy in 1967. They voted to kill him.

To see what the "new" Mississippi is like—how it has changed and how it has not—a good place to start is Joseph Williams' farm.

You drive out from Greenville with Rims Barber, the Delta Ministry staffer who has been coming to Yazoo since spring 1967. For seventy miles the country is flat, and

Highway 12 stretches hot and straight between the cotton rows.

Rims is wiry, intense, bespectacled; he has worn a mustache ever since a *National Observer* reporter described him in print as a "militant Wally Cox." A Presbyterian minister in Mississippi since 1964, he has been coming to Yazoo at the request of the Yazoo County Voters League, a loose organization of Negro leaders in the rural districts.

"The league had already registered about five hundred Negro voters," Rims says. "Since then we've hired three people, and they've registered another five hundred voters. The whites have a total of maybe six hundred registered."

You think for a minute about the implications of this. Yazoo is the county the Meredith Marchers considered most dangerous when they were planning their route toward Jackson a year earlier.

It's Yazoo County that operates two separate Neighborhood Youth Corps—one white and one Negro—with federal money. Yazoo, thirteen years after the Supreme Court's school desegregation ruling, still didn't have one black kid or one black teacher in a school with whites. The county didn't have a single Negro deputy, policeman, or elected official.

The county seat sits on a hill, the first hill in seventy miles, a surprise jutting up from the sea of cotton on the eastern boundary of the Delta. It's not a comfortable town to drive through; there are too many stories about Yazoo City to make any civil rights worker at ease there. Rims has been trying for months to rent a house there, but people are afraid, and even many of the DM staff don't think he ought to take the chance.

You pull to a stop in an Esso station in the Negro part of town—you can tell by the dirt streets, even if you couldn't see any people—and Rims gives fair warning: "Last indoor toilet you'll see today." You take the hint, and in a few minutes the car, tank full, is swooping down the long green hill back into the Delta.

"We're coming up on Eden," Rims says after a while as the speedometer needle drops down through seventy. "This was a Klan place, and for a long time we couldn't register a soul around here. But when one plantation broke, then all the folks went. They figured the planters couldn't fire them all."

And suddenly you're going up, out of the Delta. You come to the top of a long, steep hill, where two men and a woman are picking cotton by hand.

"Joseph Williams' place is next," says Rims, and points to a tree where Williams' three hundred acres start. In the six miles since you left Eden, you have seen two houses and three human beings.

"He's out in the field," Mrs. Williams says after you've parked in front of the farmhouse and assured the dog of your friendly attitude. "I'll fetch him."

But Rims tells her you'll go yourself, needing the chance to stretch. You walk past a hog lot, a pen of baby chicks, a vegetable table garden, a pair of cows tied to a tree, and several hissing geese, and through a little woods to the field where he's working.

Joseph Williams waves, finishes a row, cuts the engine, and climbs down off the tractor to say hello.

The man who wants to be Yazoo County's second Negro supervisor—the first was elected during Reconstruction one hundred years ago—is slender, six feet two inches tall, with the straight bearing of a man who's been in the army.

"Yes," he says as you all walk back to the house. "I was in North Africa, and Sicily, and Anzio, and Red Beach. They still had us segregated in those days, you know, but I was with the first Negro outfit that saw action."

Mrs. Williams, plump and smiling, invites you into the

living room. A little shy with a stranger, she fusses over Rims, who obviously is an honored guest.

You continue to ask Williams about his World War II service. "Yes, it made a difference in the way we felt," he says. "One afternoon in a place called Bear Ridge our whole company was pinned down from one o'clock till four o'clock, and when it was over, there were five of us left who weren't dead or wounded.

"When you go through that," he said, "you somehow come back expecting to get a fair deal at home."

And what did they find?

Joseph Williams leans back on the couch and grins.

"We got back here to Camp Shelby and there were the signs—'Negro Here' and 'White Here.' You see, on the way over, they let us mix up all we wanted. Coming back they started to split us back up.

"Now the bunch I was with didn't like that. They'd been at the front for two years.

"So we went in the place marked 'White Here' and ordered some coffee. The girl didn't want to wait on us, but she finally did, and then she went and got the MP's.

"The MP's came, and they told us we couldn't eat there, but there were about twelve or fourteen of us, and we was feeling kind of mad, so they left us alone. After a while the colonel came, and he said, 'Now, boys, I don't like this any more than you do, but that's the way it is. You're back home now.'

"So we got up and left."

Soon after he got out, he says, he bought this farm—and the first of the four bad times began.

"The real estate man really didn't intend for me to pay for this place," he says. "I had a little money he saw waving around, and he was intending to get that—thought I was gonna be ready to move in a year or so."

It was a white neighborhood, Williams explains. Though

the farms are large and the houses isolated, it bothered the neighbors—all of them white—that a Negro had moved in. "All at once they tightened down. They went to killing my stock. Or they would steal it. Trying to get me discouraged.

"They did that for about two years. And then they lightened up."

After those first two years they let him pretty much alone. He even traded work with the nearest neighbor, going down to help if he got behind; the neighbor would return the favor if Williams was running behind.

But in 1958 the "bottom fell out again."

"I joined the N-double-A-C-P. And they didn't want none of that in here. They had already run it out of Yazoo City and run the officers out of town."

Sheriff Hood, Williams says, stopped him one night on the way home from Yazoo City. He made all three occupants of the car get out to be searched.

"When he seen that little old NAACP button the preacher had on, he got rough. He said, 'I got in mind to kill you all now.' And he called the other police—five more police—and four civilians.

"He taken us down to city hall—that's when it wasn't too comfortable down there—and started to ask us, 'Where you been?' I said I had been to a meeting.

"He said, 'I know. We followed you all the way from Jackson.'"

After searching through all the papers in a briefcase Williams carried and threatening all three prisoners, the police finally let them go, but kept the papers.

"The next morning," Mr. Williams recalls, "the man I been buying gas from ever since '49 came out and got his tank. 'Don't want your business no more,' he said.

"I couldn't say anything, because it was his. So then he froze out all the other gas companies. I couldn't get no more gas. So all right. That same tractor you saw me on today—it was new then. I drove it up out there under that tree, went to the sale and got me a pair of mules. And I went to farming then with mules.

"That went on for three or four years. And then they let me up again."

When he pauses, you look around the spotless room. Plaques, "Honor Thy Father and Mother" and "The Gift of God is Eternal Life," hang on the papered walls. A rifle is mounted above the side door; Rims follows your gaze and smiles. "And that isn't the only gun in this room." Among wedding and army pictures on a chest of drawers is a white button with red letters: "We Try Harder."

"The next big trouble started when James Meredith went to that school," Joseph Williams says.

"Way down in the night, about one o'clock, my white neighbor called me from out on the road. He says, 'Joe!' I was back there in the bedroom. I says, 'Suh?'

" 'Come here!' Well, I jumped, you know, I thought he needed help. Hadn't of been him, I wouldn't have went out. I knew the others was on me, but him and me was just good neighbors.

"So when I went out there, him and his son was out there. He had an automatic shotgun. The others was waiting up the road. But he never did put it down on me. He kept it pointed up in the air. And he come just a-cussin', see. 'I thought maybe one time we could let you live around here, but we can't.'

" 'Yessir, yessir,' you know, and he cursed.

"So after while—my wife was back there sleeping—she came to the door there, and she could hear him, you know, so she went back in. She got this here small gun and my rifle.

"See, by him facing me, well, he didn't see her behind him until she got close enough to him, you know, to touch him. She said, 'Drop that gun.' Now if you noticed, my wife, she stutters. And when she commenced a-stutterin' and he looked back, that gun's what he looked back in. I was afraid she was going to shoot him before she could tell him what she wanted!"

Amid the shouts of laughter from the front room, a voice is heard from the kitchen, where pans have been rattling. "You makin' fun of me out there again?"

"Well," Joseph Williams goes on, "I told her, 'Don't. Don't shoot him.' Well, he dropped the gun all right.

"I picked it up and give it back to him. I said, 'I never would have thought you would have did me that way, Mr. A———.'"

It turned out that the white farmers had decided Joseph Williams was solely responsible for the attempts to integrate Ole Miss. After all, Joseph Williams was president of the Yazoo County NAACP, and everybody was sure it was the NAACP that was backing James Meredith. But as Joseph and his neighbor talked, the crowd down the road drifted away. And finally the neighbor turned to go. "Don't tell nobody I come down," he said, and he and his son walked on down the dirt road.

"That didn't mean they didn't tighten down on me again," Joseph Williams recalls. "First of all they wouldn't sell you nothing—not even food. And you would try to get food through somebody else, and they find that out, and they'd pressure them.

"And they wouldn't gin your cotton. And they wouldn't sell you gas again. I had paid for this place. I didn't owe anything on it, but I owed $1700 on that tractor. And the banker called me in. He says, 'You got to pay up.'

"I says, 'Mr. Taylor, I paid you this year's note. I don't owe you anything else.' I says, 'I don't believe you treatin' me right.'

"And so we talked on for a while. He tried to play hard.

Then he said, 'Joe, I told them that.' He says, 'I was *told* to close you out. But I told them you was going to be pretty hard to close out.'

"So then he decided to let me go.

"Well, in March, I had sold the timber on this place, about 250 acres of it. The man started cutting the timber. He cut three or four loads, and they found out he was on here and they told him, 'You can't buy that timber—that's civil rights land.' And he had to quit. He paid me a hundred dollars and said, 'That's the best I can do. They won't let me buy it.' And so I been here twenty years, and this timber hasn't been sold.

"Then they decided they wasn't going to gin my cotton. So I went to a place called Medway. I went to the gin just like nothing happened, drove up under the sucker. I seen people watching me, you know—well, they went on and ginned mine.

"When they got through ginning, when they gave me the ticket, the owner wrote me a note, says 'You can gin all you make.' So from then on I ginned there.

"Now I couldn't buy anything in his store. But when they called him in to question about ginning, he said, 'I run a public gin, and if I don't gin his cotton, if he's got sense enough he can pull a suit against me.'

"But there were other farmers couldn't get their cotton ginned, and they left the county."

Many of the men with families, Williams says, just couldn't take the pressure. People who belonged to civil rights organizations were even asked to take their savings out of the banks in Yazoo City; the banks wouldn't handle the accounts any more.

"Well, that went on for a year or so, then they lightened up some. But then this March, I decided to run for supervisor from Beat Four. That's where it started all over again, only worse."

Harry Bowie discussing voter registration and campaign organization with local leaders (*Nash Basom*)

Every Mississippi county is divided into five beats (the name for the districts is a leftover from the days when plantation owners took turns on night patrol to keep the slaves in line). The board of supervisors—one man from each beat—runs the county.

The board levies all county taxes, sets tax rates, and sets evaluation. It builds and maintains all the county roads, and draws up the jury lists. If it wants to, the board can establish hospitals, libraries, bond issues to attract industry, parks, surplus commodities for the hungry, and Community Action Programs under the Antipoverty Act. In counties where the board doesn't want these things, they don't exist. The board hires all the road crews, oversees the sheriff's work, and can, if it wishes, authorize extra judges and constables.

Until the fall of 1967 there was not a single Negro among the state's 410 county supervisors.

"I'd been thinking about running for about eight years,"

Joseph Williams says, "if we got enough people registered. So this spring when it looked like we would have enough registered, I put the rumor out that I was thinking about running.

"That's where it started all over again.

"Mr. Anderson, the store owner that lives up there by the present supervisor, he said, 'Joe? What is all this talk about you running for supervisor?' I say, 'I don't know, Mr. Harris, sir.'

"He had my account all added up. He said, 'If you gonna run, I want my money. But if you ain't gonna run, I'll let you have anything you want.' Well, we talked on there awhile, and he says, 'What you gonna do?'

"I say, 'Oh, I believe I'll run, Mr. Harris.'

"He says, 'Look, don't you know you ain't gonna have no friends?' He says, 'Joe, you got many white friends, and if you gonna do that, you ain't gonna have no white friends.'"

Joseph Williams smiles. "That," he admits, "is where the devil worked in me. I said, 'Mr. Harris, you know I really

Head Start class at Kelly's Settlement, in a building provided by Vernon Dahmer (*Bruce Hilton*)

didn't know that. If I had known that, I wouldn't have run for supervisor.'

"He said, 'That's what I thought.'

"I said, 'No, sir, if I'd known I had that many white friends, I'd have run for sheriff.'

"That's when the poor man walked out of his own store."

Within twenty-four hours, there wasn't a store in the area that would sell Williams food for his family or for his animals. A Negro woman came by at night to report that her boss-man had said, "Williams better pick his casket. They sure as hell gonna kill him this time."

But, "I ain't picking no casket," he said. "That's my wife's job."

Another friend reported that he'd been offered money by a white man to burn the Williams house down. "Man, don't you act that foolish," the candidate told him. "Whoever try to burn my house, if I be there I'm going to get him.

"And I meant that," he says. "Now, I'm not gonna bother nobody. But you see a man coming pouring gas around my house and going to burn it down, am I going to say, 'Yassuh, don't burn my house'? Well, I'm going to fire on him.

"You know I was an expert marksman in the army."

Through another source, Williams learned that some of his neighbors had met to discuss killing him—and, by a narrow margin, had voted not to do so, yet. But the decision caused a split in the ranks; some of them held a rump session and voted the other way.

In August, while he was handing out election literature in the Negro section of Medway, an old man sidled up to him and warned, "Joe, they went down the road. They gonna get you when you come by."

"I said, 'Okay, thanks. I'm proud you told me.' And I went home a different way. Now those men had been drinking. But whether they was drinking or not, I wasn't going to take no whupping.

"I take cussing—they have come out there to that gate and cussed me till they got tired. I take that.

"But now if one going to hit me, I'm going to try to beat him to the draw."

Just then Mrs. Williams appears in the dining-room doorway, inviting you to some "coffee." Besides coffee the table holds rolls, goulash, beans, and sweet potato pie. The men are seated; eight-year-old Helen Williams peeks impishly from behind a curtain in one of the doorways, and Mrs. Williams retires to the kitchen. The talk turns to farming. The picture of the World War II serviceman on the wall shows that Williams is one veteran who has lost weight instead of gaining it.

"Yes"—he smiles—"I go up and down. I weigh two-twenty when the pressure's off. It's just about two hundred now."

The sound of a truck comes from the road, and nobody says anything until it pulls into the front yard and is identified as belonging to a friend.

The young man who comes in and sits at the table is an employee of one of Yazoo County's biggest industries, a factory run by a man known nationally for his "moderate" racial views.

"Well, no," the new arrival says, "I wouldn't say we were treated the same as the whites. All the Negroes but one work on the loading dock. The top pay there is just about the same as the starting pay for the men inside."

There is one man on the dock who has a college degree, he adds; another college graduate was recently promoted to belt operator, becoming the lone Negro production employee.

"Tell him where you eat," Rims Barber prompts.

"We eat where we can, when we can. Just grab a bite,

because there's no time during the shift. The whites eat inside in the cafeteria."

The sun is getting low, and it's time to leave for the Friday night meeting, but while the table is being cleared, another visitor arrives. Joseph Williams greets him like a son and introduces him as "just back from Vietnam—got wounded twice over there."

"Hey," Williams says, "you going down there tomorrow? Apply for that police job in Yazoo City?"

"I think maybe I will," the young man says. "They won't know what to do, but I think I will."

Williams explains that his visitor is a trained military policeman, not due for discharge for another ten months. Applying now will give them time to fight the rejection in the courts. "Because they will turn him down. The last colored man to go down there had been in the army thirty-three years, and the chief of police just said one word— 'never.'

"Course, there's no test to be a po-lice around here—just how bad you want to hit a colored man."

After arrangements are made to go to Yazoo City the next day, Williams feeds the animals and milks the cows. As he works, he talks about what he thinks a supervisor should be like.

"My family has been paying taxes eighty-five years on the home place, up the road a ways," he says, "but we never had a road. There's paving for the white places and dirt for the Negroes.

"If you're going to be a supervisor, be for white *and* colored. Fix your white roads just like the colored. Fix the colored roads just like you do the white. And whatever you going to give one, give the other one the same way."

Beat Four, he points out, has always had its own representative on the Farmers Home Administration committee. But it has never been a Negro. And a Negro, he says, can never get a big enough FHA loan in Yazoo County to make a real difference.

"I'd like to change that. I'd like to see the hospital opened up, and decent schools." The last time Negroes visited a white man in the white hospital in Yazoo City—the patient was the priest of the Negro Roman Catholic mission church —"two carloads of police threw them out."

By now it is pitch dark. Mrs. Williams, Helen, the two visitors, and Mr. Williams pile into Rims Barber's car. The car moves carefully down the deserted roads, through thick woods broken by patches of cleared land. There is a quick stop to see if a friend from another farm wants to go along, but the place is dark. (There would have been no way to check by phone; Southern Bell hasn't installed phones for the Negroes of Beat Four yet. "My white neighbors have had phones for twenty years," Williams says, "and I've had my application in for that long. They have the wires up to the house now. But even the Negro school doesn't have the phones yet.")

The car is heading for New Hope Baptist Church, where the Beat Four voter meetings are held on alternate Fridays. Joseph Williams has been a member there thirty-four years and a Sunday school teacher twenty years.

The church, he explains, sits in the middle of two wooded acres given the congregation during Reconstruction. "The deacons used to be afraid to hold freedom meetings here because they were afraid the building would be burned down. Then, when we decided we needed to rebuild anyway, the congregation said okay."

He described a Sunday morning when Medgar Evers, not long before his death in Jackson, came by to talk about voter registration. "We heard this car come in, and when people saw who it was, they tried to act like he wasn't there at all. They were scared to death.

"I was on the platform, and I was scared, too. But I figured if he dared to come out here, we could hear what he had to say. I went on back to the door and invited him in."

Preachers are worried about their buildings and about their standing in the white community, Williams says. They're afraid to get involved in anything that would bring about real change.

"One preacher, he said to me, 'I ain't got time for that. I'm on my way to heaven.'

"I said to him, 'We may be on our way to heaven, but we sure are catchin' a lot of hell now!' "

The car swings into a side road and comes to a stop at a gate. "The fox hunters aren't here!" Barber and Williams say in unison.

While Barber opens the gate, Williams explains. Every Friday night that a meeting is scheduled, at least two carloads of armed white men are parked by the lonely gate to the church property. They don't say anything; they just watch each person who comes in or out. "We checked," Rims says as he climbs back into the car. "They never are here on a night when there's no meeting."

"They're just out here running foxes." Joseph Williams grins. "Course, I don't ever hear no dogs."

The meeting is small—about a dozen people when everybody arrives. An elderly man who comes in late takes a front seat and whispers to his companion, "The fox hunters are out there now—they're late tonight."

Edgar Brookins, a farmer from the other end of the beat, reads from Psalm 1 and then leads in the Lord's Prayer, lining out each phrase for the group to repeat. He urges attendance at a voter rally the following Sunday in Medway, and suggests everybody try to bring at least one other person. "We been asleep a long time," he says, "but it's time to get up and be about our Father's business."

*(Ken Thompson)*

Joseph Williams adds an exhortation. "When I was this high," he says, holding his hand level with his shoulder, "and Alfred Hogue was this high"—hand at waist level—"my folks taught me to call him Mr. Hogue. Now it's time to show that we are men, too."

To Rims's embarrassment, Williams goes on at some length about the DM staffer's work. "Of all the people who have tried to help us, this man has done the most. He won't stand out in front and get the credit—he just helps us with what we want to do. He's stuck by us for months, and we know he ain't going to leave when it gets rough."

Then there is a general discussion, concentrating on Voters' League business. The items include:

"Mr. Brookins put in an acre of cucumbers this year, and if you haven't heard how it came out, you'd better talk to him. He got enough out of that acre to keep his boy in school this year. Talk to him about maybe doing the same thing. After all, part of freedom is a little money in the pocket."

"You all heard about the people on the ——— plantation getting $400 back because the man hadn't been paying one dollar an hour. Maybe you didn't know that it was the movement that got hold of the Labor Department and got the place investigated. That's your movement, and when things like this happen, you should let people know, so they won't be asking, 'What has all this agitation ever done for me?' "

Another announcement is that everybody's check for aid to dependent children will be cut four or five dollars a month, starting with the next check. "Now that's the fault of the state legislature. There was more federal money, but they refused to ask for it. Remember that when you vote."

"We need to support the S——— family. They have been thrown off three different plantations now because they tried to put their kids in the white schools. But they haven't given up."

Williams asks one of the men in the audience, who drives a school bus, how many children he carries at a time. "About ninety to ninety-five" is the answer.

"Well, it isn't right," somebody says, and the group agrees. "Our kids get crowded in like that—it's dangerous. The white kids have enough buses that they only ride thirty-five or so to a bus.

"Now, twenty-eight families have already signed up for this suit against the school board," Williams says. "If you're a parent of a schoolchild and would like to join the suit, I have the papers here."

There is more discussion, led by Mr. Brookins, of problems in the county. Plans are made for getting necessary information or seeing certain officials. An offering is taken, and the meeting is halted while the officers count out the $9.60 contributed.

Finally, at 10:30 P.M., the meeting is over. You crawl

back into the car, where Helen has already fallen asleep on her mother's shoulder, clutching her rag doll.

The cars move out of the woods in single file, close together, but the fox hunters have gone home. The group in the car is silent for a while as they wind back over the hills toward the farm. It is Joseph Williams who breaks the silence.

"Yes, I get tired of all this worrying sometimes. But things have got to be better, and this is the only way to make it so."

He looks over his shoulder at his wife and little girl asleep in the corner of the back seat. "If I don't do this," he says, "that kid there'll have to go through the same thing."

Since Joe Williams came home from the war, Mississippi has gone through many changes. Most of the change came between 1964 and 1968—but not always for the better.

There is more freedom to speak now. Whereas a mild statement against violence had once cost a score of ministers their pulpits, a few white clergymen now work openly with the Delta Ministry and the Freedom Democratic Party. An uneasy coalition that includes white planters, liberal newspapermen, conservative blacks, grass-roots organizers, and old-time FDP types tried to make itself felt through the regular Democratic party machinery; when this failed, they held their own convention and elected a biracial delegation that was seated at Chicago. Four years earlier, the whites and many of the blacks in the delegation had shunned the FDP attempt to challenge Senator Eastland at the Democratic convention.

Local politics have changed, too. In a few counties—heavily Negro—white candidates for re-election have been observed going from door to door in black neighborhoods, promising paved streets and a sewer line in return for votes.

The powerful men who opposed the entry of poverty programs in 1965 are now on the boards of Community Action Projects, training programs, and housing projects. They found that they couldn't stop the programs—but they could control them.

There are signs that the state is coming out of the nineteenth century. In 1967, women began serving on Mississippi juries for the first time. Prohibition was repealed in 1966. The sovereignty commission, which was originally set up to funnel $100,000 of state tax money each year into the White Citizens' Councils, found itself under question in the state legislature. And the state legislature, which until mid-1967 had prohibited black men from even sitting in the visitors' gallery, suddenly found itself with a black member, Robert Clark of Holmes County.

But the legislature has refused twice since 1965 to enact a compulsory school law to replace the one it repealed after the Supreme Court's desegregation decision in 1954. And the state still pays most of the tuition for any child whose parents choose to send him to a private segregated school operated by the Citizens' Council.

Violence has not diminished much; four churches were burned in the summer of 1968, and three homes were bombed. But these events didn't get much publicity, because the rest of the country didn't care.

Suddenly confronted with the fact that there really is not much difference between Mississippi and their own states, many of the most vociferous northern champions of the Mississippi struggle have lost interest. Aware for the first time that an indictment of Mississippi is an accusation against their own unjust (though more subtle and sophisticated) systems, northerners became apathetic.

Others, after a brief stint of concern for Mississippi, have turned their attention to newer headlines. Students who might have come to Mississippi in 1964 are now in the northern ghetto or demonstrating against the Vietnam war. As attention has faltered, so has support; six of us were cut from the Delta Ministry staff within a year because of lack of funds.

For the people whose lives had been spent on the plantations, 1967 was worse than 1964. The minimum wage law finally went into effect (for a meager dollar an hour) in early 1967, and planters responded by trimming their work force back to the bare minimum. The state estimated that the sixty thousand cotton choppers of 1959 had dwindled to two thousand in 1966.

Three teams of doctors toured the Delta in 1967, and all —even the one sent out by Governor Johnson to "answer" the other—found widespread nutritional deficiencies. In Marshall County, 300 children attending Head Start were examined; 270 were found to have anemia caused by hunger. The Freedom Movement had made it possible for these people to vote and in some cases to get surplus food or food stamps from a truculent Department of Agriculture. But it had only begun to work at the basic problems.

Senators Joseph Clark and Robert Kennedy also visited the Delta that year, stopping unannounced at plantation

Owen Brooks, DM associate director, and Dr. King during a Meredith March break (*Nash Basom*)